"Michael Edwards is a distinguished literary critic and himself a fine poet. In *Untimely Christianity*, he offers an acutely discerning reflection on the conscience-searing language of Jesus and the startling otherness of the words of biblical poetry from the psalms, prophets, and sayings of Christ. I know of no comparable introduction to authentic reading of the Bible—indeed, this little book, small in size but enormous in consequence, is a must-read for anyone who seeks to understand the Bible as the distinctive word of God."

—David Lyle Jeffrey, author of *Scripture and the English Poetic Imagination* and Distinguished Senior Fellow, Baylor Institute for Studies in Religion

"Michael Edwards reminds us that it is dangerous to read the Bible. His piercingly beautiful essay restores the surprising strangeness of the text. I was moved and disturbed and felt often I was experiencing the full reality of Scripture for the first time. We desperately need people with Professor Edwards's poetic and philosophical skill to awaken us from rationalist readings to experience the Person who haunts the text. The meditation on the nature of translation as a spiritual practice was particularly insightful, and the work itself owes some of its power to the fact that it is the work of an Englishman, writing in French, and then ably translated by John Marson Dunaway. I learned so much: about the Lord's Prayer as poetry, the relation of faith to reality, and the potency of church architecture and ancient stones alike to prompt us to believe in the existence of a world 'that responds to this aspiration and this reserve.' Christians will find their faith made startlingly strange, while nonbelievers will be beguiled by this elegant, nonpietistic presentation of the compelling nature of faith."

—the Rev'd Canon Alison Grant Milbank, author of *God and the Gothic* and professor of theology and literature, University of Nottingham

"Eureka! Michael Edwards's pungent, wise, and simple book on how Christianity interrupts and reorders our lives is now available for English readers. If you want to know what the Bible says about knowing God, about faith, hope, and joy; if you want to read some of the best pages ever written on the Lord's Prayer; if, in short, you want to know how to *hear* the Bible, read this book."

—Kevin Hart, author of *Barefoot: Poems* and
Edwin B. Kyle Professor of Christian Studies,
University of Virginia

"Echoes of Pascal and Claudel sound through this fresh and profound meditation on the meaning of the gospel. Edwards's book challenges us to embark upon a more authentic search for the truth about our humanity and our plight in this world through a fresh encounter with the Bible. He takes us through the Bible as a disciple with a poet's eye so as to discern and unpack its all-too-familiar passages through attentiveness to the poetry of its words, images, and sentence patterns. Not just the parables and psalms but most major teachings and stories show themselves to have a depth that demands a greater awareness of the art of the expression and the mystery contained therein. The chapter on the Our Father is a tour de force that shows the reader how a more careful look at the pattern and meaning of words opens up the teaching of Christ as a surprising and compelling account of human existence in relation to God. While many now speak of the 'evangelization of culture,' as if faith and culture were always at odds, Edwards shows that the Bible, the good news, is already an active source of human culture and a wellspring of poetry and art. Of course, numerous poets, artists, and composers have testified to this fact. Edwards's *Untimely Christianity* is a reminder and a stimulus for a true cultural renewal of Christian inspiration in our day."

—John P. Hittinger, author of *The Vocation of a Catholic Philosopher* and director of the St. John Paul II Institute,
University of St. Thomas, Houston

UNTIMELY CHRISTIANITY

Untimely Christianity

Hearing the Bible in a Secular Age

Michael Edwards

Translated by
John Marson Dunaway

Foreword by
Alister McGrath

Fortress Press
Minneapolis

UNTIMELY CHRISTIANITY
Hearing the Bible in a Secular Age

Translated by John Marson Dunaway from the French
Pour un christianisme intempestif (Fallois, 2020).

Cover design: Kris Miller

Print ISBN: 978-1-5064-8087-9
eBook ISBN: 978-1-5064-8088-6

In memory of
Dallas A. Willard (1935–2013)

"Do you know God?"
—"Only by name."

Contents

Foreword

The Bible stands at the heart of Christian faith and devotion, a treasure chest of wisdom that resources both the church and individual believers in their journeys of faith and ministries. Yet many, including myself, often find themselves trapped within conventional ways of reading the Bible, which blunt our sense of excitement in engaging the text, often creating a sense of "sameness," even staleness. Every now and then, however, a work appears that breathes fresh air into our reading of the Bible. As I read Michael Edwards's *Untimely Christianity*, I found myself reading biblical passages I thought I knew well in new ways—ways that opened up new horizons of understanding and engagement. Edwards is not demanding that we change our theology; rather, he is asking us to allow the Bible to speak to us freshly so that we can hear its distinctive voice with a new clarity.

I came away invigorated and refreshed from my reading of *Untimely Christianity*. It was as if someone had opened a window into a deeper and more reflective approach to the text, which left

me satisfied and excited at one and the same time. Edwards's way
of engaging the text often led to insights that I already knew—but
they were set out in a fresh way that allowed me to see and appre-
ciate them anew, as if I were seeing them for the first time. I hope
that many will find that Edwards's short book, so sympathetically
translated by John Dunaway, helps them see familiar texts with
new eyes.

Alister McGrath
Oxford University

Translator's Preface

My scholarly interests throughout my career have gravitated toward Christian writers, particularly novelists, and the single most useful secondary source in my research on Christian novelists was a 1984 book by Michael Edwards (*Towards a Christian Poetics*). When I learned that he had written a book called *Bible et poésie* (2016), I was eager to read it and was not in the least disappointed. *Pour un christianisme intempestif* is yet another brilliant reflection on the countercultural power of God's word; it is indeed a privilege to make it accessible to English readers. Throughout this project, Professor Edwards has granted me the favor of meticulous attention to the details of refining the translation, always with the gentle tactfulness of a true brother. I must thank my wife, Trish, for her carefully attentive collaboration, as well as the advice of colleagues Bryan J. Whitfield, Anna Weaver, Randall Harshbarger, and Gordon Johnston. Finally, I wish to thank Alister McGrath for kindly agreeing to write the foreword.

Introduction

True Christianity

1.

Whether we are Christians or not, do we know what Christianity is? The first Christians had the feeling of entering, by faith, into a strange and new world. They understood that even faith is mysterious, a gift they had received from God. They were in a hurry, in a hurry to acquaint themselves with the new life that was opening before them and to bring to others the good news that they had heard, assuming that the end of the world was approaching and that they must redeem the little time that remained for them. Centuries later, Christianity, caught in the perspective of European rationalism, has become for nonbelievers a set of doctrines comparable to Marxism or existentialism and dependent on a useless and unfounded belief, while for believers it is very often the same set of doctrines with associated practices. Routine has set in. The modes of thought of a civilization far removed from biblical revelation veil the troubling singularity of Christianity, of its God, and of the familiar reality that it differently illumines.

We have *forgotten* the true Christianity. We must recover the Christianity of the first believers and of those who century after century and in all confessions of the church—those of Christians in Christ—have lived the same faith under the impulse of the same grace.

Léon Bloy: "There is only one sadness, and that is not to be a saint."[1] Catherine of Siena: "If you are what you are supposed to be, you will set fire to the entire world."[2] It is indeed all about *being* and *fire* when it comes to a countercultural Christianity, one that contradicts what we would naturally say in whatever place or moment.[3] Christianity cannot be listed among the various world-views or philosophies of life proposed by the successive societies of a fallen world separated from God and, absent the aid offered it by a light from elsewhere, blind. It is untimely in the first place in that it does not have to adapt to "progress" and the exigencies of each passing generation. And yet a press release about the *Revised English Bible* in 1989 assumes that "since the Bible is the sovereign guide for the Christian faith, it follows that it must respond to the various demands of the age." Over and beyond the error in logic—the guide must let itself be guided by what it is supposed to guide—even graver mistakes appear. By deciding what the age must modify in the Bible, it is the translators who become the guides, and by listening to the incessant, protean demands of fleeting epochs, the voice of fallen humanity is given a privileged status. Each modernity,

---

1 Léon Bloy, *The Woman Who Was Poor* (South Bend, IN: St. Augustine's Press, 2015).
2 Letter 368 to Stefano Maconi.
3 In Edwards's original title, the French word *intempestif* literally means "untimely." However, it also has the connotation of "countercultural." Therefore, both English translations are used in my version, as each has a slightly different connotation that is appropriate in different contexts. The subtitle, too, contains rich ambiguities. Literally, it translates as "Knowing How to Understand the Bible," but *entendre* in French also means "to hear," and Edwards often emphasizes the many Scriptures in which we are urged to "have ears to hear."

which can contain good and is never abandoned by God, is nevertheless the product of our fallenness.

But Christianity is untimely in a more radical way. It always arrives out of step, like a counterculture, and, more deeply, contrary to what our ego desires—or the part of our ego that we recognize. It is untimely from the very beginning. Jesus's teachings and the apostles' preaching seemed hardly appropriate to the Jews as well as to the "gentiles," the Jews seeing it as the absolute contradiction of their religion and the Greeks as the contradiction of their conception of the real and of their "wisdom." Christianity was so out of place in Jerusalem, in Athens, and in Rome that Jesus himself, and the first Christians in great numbers, was killed for having troubled the "hallucinated order" of the world.[4] How far away that all seems in our supposedly Christianized countries, where our Christian religion, as our churches, are part of the landscape. We must relearn the untimeliness of salvation, the otherness of the gospel word, and consider it a barbarian language and the great disruptor of our lives and habits.

Christians, we must remove the all too familiar appearance from Christianity and recognize its surprising strangeness. Unbelievers, we can acknowledge that among the first listeners to what was being presented, after all, as "good news," some felt a bizarre desire to listen and change—surprisingly discovering that it was their deepest desire, that quite unexpectedly it was precisely what they were waiting for—and that the gospel continues to repulse and attract.

---

4   Edwards is adapting a phrase from René Char's poem "D'un même lieu," in *Dans la pluie giboyeuse* (Paris: Gallimard, 1968).

2.

Who is God? In what world are we living? Who am I? What does it mean to be a Christian? To live as a Christian? Such are the slightly crazy questions that must now be posed again, and doubtless over and over ceaselessly. And where will the answers be found? In the Bible.[5] But how many think this spontaneously, even among those who recognize that the Bible is the word of God? How easily does the idea interpose itself that it is better to consult the commentators and theologians! Theologians' help is precious (except when they start speculating and adding, taking the Bible for raw material that needs to be worked on), but why not inquire directly at the source before asking for help? Otherwise, it is as if we were reading Flaubert scholars instead of Flaubert himself. The great theologians on the New Testament are Matthew, Mark, Luke, John, Paul, James, Peter, Jude, and the author of the Epistle to the Hebrews, and it is in their company that we should listen to and meditate on Revelation.

For the Bible is different. Pascal writes that a certain style surprises us: "One expects to see an author and one finds a man."[6] Of the Bible, we could say, "One expects to see authors and one finds God." In the heart of the texts, a living word makes itself heard; behind the absence of authors, a divine presence makes itself felt. It is a privilege to read the Bible, a great, fearful, and joyous adventure of our being. It suffices to read it attentively and with precision, without preconceived notions, for us to feel its authority; to read it constantly, through a vital need as important as air in our lungs, for us to understand and accept its magisterium.[7] But how difficult

---

5 Edwards normally cites the French translation of the Jerusalem Bible but sometimes also La Bible de Port-Royal. My translation cites the King James Version unless otherwise noted.

6 Pascal, *Pensées* (1670), ed. L. Brunschvicg (Paris: Hachette, 1909), sect. 1, no. 29.

7 *Magisterium*, while a familiar term for Catholics, may not be easily recognizable for Protestants. It refers to the theological authority that resides in the teaching of the Roman Catholic Church, whereas Edwards is suggesting that such authority resides in Scripture.

it is to allow this magisterium to be accomplished in us! Force of habit turns our thoughts away from it. If we are reflecting on a question of doctrine or practice, do we not seek the answer elsewhere? Just to take one example, how do we persuade nonbelievers of God's demands and the infinite joy of salvation? Instead of studying the way Jesus and the apostles proceeded, do we not turn to apologetics—a method long elaborated by our reasonings and *which is there*, like a self-evident answer? Before a transcendent God and before his revelation—which charges us to listen, to understand according to our capacity, and to act—all our structures of thought, as certainly all our interpretations, risk becoming idols. By defending them, it is not God we are serving but ourselves.

And Bible reading can forever surprise and stun us—can just as well surprise and stun authentic Christians who do not recognize themselves in the humdrum version of Christianity over which I was grieving at the beginning of this reflection. At the outset of his preaching ministry, Jesus spoke in the synagogue at Capernaum, and his listeners "were astonished at his doctrine" (Mark 1:22): *exeplèssonto*, which is translated in French as "étaient stupéfaits" and "abasourdis" and in various English versions as "amazed," "astonished," and "astounded." Let us say they were "speechless, dumbstruck" and ask ourselves if Jesus's words produce in us the same kind of awestruck wonder. We could equivocate by concluding that they were astonished less by the content of his teaching than by his manner of speaking, "for," writes Mark, "he taught them as one that had authority, and not as the scribes." However, to the Sadducees who are trying to confound him by posing a sardonic question on the resurrection, Jesus responds, "'Ye do err, not knowing the scriptures, nor the power of God. . . . Have ye not read that which was spoken unto you by God, saying, I am the God of Abraham, and the God of Isaac, and the God of Jacob? God is not the God of the dead, but of the living. And when the multitude heard this, they were astonished at his doctrine" (Matthew 22:29–33). Our weakness is in no longer being astonished. Christianity, having become familiar, reputed to be the home of numerous "Christian" countries in the heart of an entire "Christian" civilization, no longer resembles that wise "foolishness" that animated the first Christians. It no longer shakes us; even atheists think they know what it is about.

We live in a fallen world, where revelation enters as an overwhelming alterity. We seek to deny this fallenness by finding less somber explanations of evil, sickness, and death. We are ignorant of God's love and humor. Reread the account of the fall. The serpent announces to the woman an intoxicating but misleading future. The day when you eat of the forbidden fruit, "your eyes shall be opened, and ye shall be as gods" (Genesis 3:5). In trying to divinize our nature, we have degraded it. To this news that turns out to be bad, the good news of the gospel responds with an announcement that is similar but far more extravagant. I pray that Christ may dwell in you by faith, Paul writes to the Ephesians, "that ye might be filled with all the fullness of God" (Ephesians 3:19). God promises much more than the serpent, whose offer seems, by comparison, rather meager. Is not God's promise, which marvelously surpasses all understanding, indeed astonishing?

Sinners in a fallen world, it is as if we were sleeping. We do not see the world as it is; we are ignorant of our own nature, what transcends nature is hidden from us. Thoreau writes in *Walden*, "I have never yet met a man who was quite awake. How could I have looked him in the face?"[8] Indeed, such an encounter would be singularly humiliating. That is also how Zechariah describes what it is like to have visions of true reality: "And the angel that talked with me

---

8 Henry David Thoreau, *Walden: A Fully Annotated Edition* (New Haven, CT: Yale University Press, 2004), 88.

came again, and waked me, as a man that is wakened out of his sleep and said unto me, 'What seest thou?'" (Zechariah 4:1–2). To awaken would be to see spiritual, celestial reality, which surrounds and supports us.

3.

For this it would take a Copernican revolution in our way of envisioning Christianity, a Copernican revolution with the Son at the center—starting with a rereading of the Bible, which reserves untimely surprises for us on all its pages. Speaking to his Father, Jesus says of his disciples, "These things I speak in the world, that they might have my joy fulfilled in themselves" (John 17:13). Does the unbeliever realize that it is the very joy of Christ, of the Son of God, that he is invited to know? Do Christians realize that they can not only share that joy but have it *in its totality*? Have we experienced that inexplicable kindness of God, that intimacy with Jesus that is able to renew us absolutely? If only . . . if we had that joy in us, through fraternal communion we would go beyond the quarrel among Catholics, Orthodox, and Protestants with their loads of errors and suspicions; our presentation of the gospel would accomplish our mission, which is to transform the world, to "turn the world upside down" (Acts 17:6).

Take also a few passages from the writings of Saint Paul. This calm affirmation, for example, for the Christians at Colossae: "Ye are dead, and your life is hid with Christ in God" (Colossians 3:3). Dead? A life hidden in God? Unheard of! Or this, two verses earlier: "Ye then [are] risen with Christ." A fact to remember every morning? Or "For me to live is Christ" (Philippians 1:21). Or "If the Spirit of him that raised up Jesus from the dead dwell in you" (Romans 8:11). Or again, "Ye are the body of Christ" (1 Corinthians 12:27). The Bible is a continuous questioning of the reader and a prodigious expansion of reality. If one listens to such words, they cease to convey notions that are a bit abstract or matters of doctrine—things one believes, and nothing more, because they are a part of Christianity—and become facts of existence, inexhaustible, no doubt weakly realized, implausibly joyous.

"True life is absent," wrote Rimbaud.[9] Yes, and it is here that it must be lived.

---

9 Rimbaud, *A Season in Hell* (1873).

1

Know That I Am God

1.

To write about God, doubtless, is folly. We are neither prophets nor apostles, so who are we to meddle? Still, if we seriously want to recover true Christianity, the knowledge of God and the recognition of his nature certainly constitute the heart of the quest and end of the journey. Once again, we have no need for the concepts of our philosophy, for the reasonings of our theology, in order to approach God through intelligence, for he has revealed himself throughout the Bible. We must hope that in listening attentively to him, our folly will disappear in the great and foolish wisdom of those to whom this revelation was confided.

The notion of the *sacred* has already encouraged the return to the God of the Bible. But such as it was put into circulation by Rudolf Otto's great book *Das Heilige* (*The Idea of the Holy*) in 1917, it has also hindered it. The presuppositions that caused this work to go astray still being current, it is better to point them out before proceeding.

Noting that a certain kind of orthodoxy had sought to rationalize Christianity to the point of rendering the idea of God exclusively rational, Otto proposes to demonstrate the irrational dimension of God, that by which God escapes the grasp of our concepts. To this end, he explores the experience of the sacred, which he presents as both a terrifying and attractive totally other, existing at the basis of all religions. Here is the first problem: As a specialist in comparative religion, Otto seems to believe in the existence of a kind of sacred-in-itself, whereas every intuition of the sacred is an intuition of the one true God. This affirmation comes not from me but from Saint Paul. Thinking of those who are not acquainted with the revelation afforded the Hebrews, he declares they cannot be forgiven for not having perceived in the works of God since the creation of the world "his eternal power and Godhead" (Romans 1:20). When Seneca, in his *Letters to Lucilius*, says he senses in a wood of ancient trees of extraordinary proportions, in the immense shadow they cast in broad daylight, in the solitude of the place, that "a God is there" (letter 41), we must believe that the Creator God grants him that thrill. When the Egyptians sculpt gods that are totally other in their immensity, they are not discovering *the sacred*, and they are worshipping still less the true God such as he demands to be known and served; they are touching with the soul's finger the eternal power and divinity of a God that they are unable to identify. On the path to conversion, the intuition of the sacred in nature or in the mystery of the invisible may strike us (we must not limit, we cannot even imagine, the ways God chooses to come to us), but this sacred is already his veiled presence.

Otto is thinking according to the European philosophical tradition instead of meditating from the outset on the biblical revelation. Whence a second problem: Justly convinced that God is found beyond our reason, Otto nonetheless feels the need at the same time to consider him rational. Seeing that God's being remains obscure, he seeks despite all this to catch him in the net of our ways of thinking. He assumes that a process of rationalization is already at work in the Bible, beginning with "the religion of Moses" and culminating in the preachings of the prophets and the gospel. Judeo-Christianity would have evolved toward "rational predicates"—God's love or his mercy—that would make him understandable. But how curious it is to call love, mercy, and forbearance rational. He judges that in Isaiah's revelation, God, whose alterity is revealed in his oft-repeated title of "The Holy One of Israel," is at the same time a "clearly conceived" God, thanks to certain of those predicates: "omnipotence, goodness, wisdom, and truth." But what do these biblical ways of naming the attributes of God have to do with the terms of our philosophy, capable, according to the first paragraph of the book, of "grasping divinity" with precision—that is, reason, teleological will, unity of essence, self-consciousness?[1]

And do we really understand them? These are more familiar notions than holiness, but *God*'s goodness and *God*'s wisdom elude our grasp because of their infinite dimension. Since God's thoughts are not our thoughts (Isaiah 55:8), *his* love, *his* justice, *his* compassion invite us into a world that is, strictly speaking, divine. By the same token, the simplest statement of the gospel, such as Paul offers it to the Corinthians—namely, "that Christ died for our sins according to the scriptures, and that he was buried, and that he rose again the third day according to the scriptures" (1 Corinthians 15:3–4)—defies reason from start to finish.

This is not a matter of semantics. The opposition of rational and irrational, which has a meaning for our way of conceiving the

---

1   Rudolf Otto, *The Idea of the Holy*, trans. John W. Harvey (Oxford: Oxford University Press, 1950), 76.

work of the spirit and envisioning the real, does not come from the Bible and does not correspond to its worldview. Thinking with the concepts and terminology of our culture inclines us inevitably to read the Bible wrongly. And if Otto describes God as "that essence irreducible to the rational, which is hidden from all philosophical study" (a door opening to a correct approach to God, but one that he closes partly), if he affirms that rationalization does not in any way eliminate the numinous, the mysterious, then speaking of the rational and irrational dimensions of God skews the data, and his manner of presenting rationalization proves dangerous. He imagines that in the "Bible the rational element is found at the forefront" and that therefore "it is the Bible that convinces us that the rational predicates . . . exhaust the essence of divinity." The Bible would be divided against itself? And there is worse still. The misleading impression given by the Bible would be inevitable, through the fault of language. All language would have "the essential purpose of transmitting notions, and the more clear and unequivocal the expressions, the better the language." Otto's simplistic idea of language is less worrisome than his distant attitude toward the Scriptures and the word they transmit.

According to the Bible, God does not elude our grasp by his irrational qualities while allowing us to understand the rational ones. He makes us sense the difference of his divinity; he approaches us. When he offers himself to us in his love, compassion, and humility, he remains himself, other, and sacred. At the very moment when he comes into our world, in Jesus, "a multitude of the heavenly host" appears suddenly to the shepherds, saying, "Glory to God in the highest, and on earth peace, good will toward men" (Luke 2:13–14)! At the same time, it reveals in a few words the ungraspable glory of God in which he remains and the love and peace that he pours lavishly out on us.

2.

In the Old Testament, encounters with God or with his messenger are so well known that we may fail to realize just how absolutely strange they are. Moses looks at the impossible in the burning bush that is not consumed (Exodus 3:2). Informed that the place where he is standing is "holy ground" (Exodus 3:5), he plants his bare feet on a *here* that has become other. When God reveals his name, he discovers the alterity of religious fear and veils his face (3:6). And if "the angel of the Lord" appears to him "from the midst of a bush" (3:2), it is God who calls him "from the midst of a bush" (3:4). How shall we explain the relationship between the angel and God, their apparent identities, which God alone understands?

A few verses suffice to draw us into the fearsome numinosity of the scene, of the intervention of heaven into an earthly place, of the Eternal into passing time. The mystery changes in the passage from the book of Joshua that recalls that encounter:

> And it came to pass, when Joshua was by Jericho, that he lifted up his eyes and looked, and, behold, there stood a man over against him with his sword drawn in his hand: and Joshua went unto him, and said unto him, "Art thou for us, or for our adversaries?" And he said, "Nay; but as captain of the host of the Lord am I now come." And Joshua fell on his face to the earth, and did worship, and said unto him, "What saith my Lord unto his servant?" And the captain of the Lord's host said unto Joshua, "Loose thy shoe from off thy foot; for the place whereon thou standest is holy." And Joshua did so. (Joshua 5:13–15)

Joshua falls into that same abyss of the unknown, but from the very ordinary. He only sees a man; he quite naturally advances toward him to find out whether he is friend or foe to his people, and when he hears the answer, either God opens his eyes so he can see the archangel or else the latter strips himself of his human appearance. Joshua too enters the frightening world of the sacred, and the first order he receives obliges him to realize it.

A third encounter, again well known, concerns Isaiah:

> In the year that king Uzziah died I saw also the Lord sitting
> upon a throne, high and lifted up, and his train filled
> the temple. . . .
> And [the seraphim] cried one unto another, and said,
> Holy, holy, holy, is the Lord of hosts.
> The whole earth is full of his glory. . . .
> Then said I,
> Woe is me! for I am undone;
> because I am a man of unclean lips,
> and I dwell in the midst of a people of unclean lips:
> for mine eyes have seen the King, the Lord of hosts.
> (Isaiah 6:1–5)

Isaiah finds himself without any transition in the presence of God, a blinding vision of an incommensurable Reality. He also sees supernatural creatures who in their praise stress in impenetrable words the unfathomable nature of God. They go from *holiness*, which names what he is in himself, to the *glory* of his being in its radiance. Already seized with astonishment in observing that God's train *fills* the temple, he realizes as well that his glory *fills* (same verb in the text) the whole earth.

His famous reaction—"Woe is me, for I am undone"—is blinding to the reader. Isaiah finds himself not in the presence of the love or the goodness or the mercy of God but facing God in all his Godhead, beyond all we know and all human conception.

Isaiah's terror is understandable, but it is surprising to note that the vision of a holy God reveals to him also his sinful condition as "a man with unclean lips." A true encounter with God is enough for this condition to grip us with horror. He understands at the same instant that his people also have "unclean lips," as if such an encounter revealed to him the fall and its disastrous consequences. Or as if such an encounter caused the fall and its disastrous consequences to appear.

3.

The word *holy* escapes us. What it designates in God remains infinitely obscure. Even while declaring that he delivers his people and keeps his covenant forever, the author of Psalm 111 adds "holy and reverend is his name." The second adjective gives information about the first; the Port-Royal Bible translates it as "Holy and terrible" (following the Vulgate, "Sanctum et terribile"); the New English Bible (NEB) as "Holy . . . and inspiring awe." God is *reverend, terrible, awesome.* And incomparable: "There is none holy as the Lord," says Hannah in her canticle (1 Samuel 2:2).

And here, it seems to me, is the passage we should read and meditate on if we want to know who he is and how to approach him: "Be still, and know that I am God" (Psalm 46:10). We must forget our questions, our conjectures, we must calm ourselves, concentrate, wait, in order to be penetrated with the simple, overwhelming idea that God is indeed God. He loves us, he seeks us, he pardons us, he allows us to serve him, but he remains above all, in heaven and in eternity, God. And what does the context say?

> Come, behold the works of the Lord,
> what desolations he hath made in the earth.
> He maketh wars to cease unto the end of the earth;

he breaketh the bow, and cutteth the spear in sunder;
he burneth the chariot in the fire.
Be still, and know that I am God:
I will be exalted among the heathen, I will be exalted in
    the earth.

(Psalm 46:8–10)

The voice of God *intervenes* in the poem. One would say the poet suddenly encounters a God-who-is-God in the act of writing. God's words are not addressed to him; he is only the mouthpiece for them, but how he must tremble in writing them!

4.

The God of the New Testament, as Otto correctly saw, is no less fearsome than the Old Testament God. The idea that a primitive, terrifying God would have changed himself into a God of love and mercy under the influence of an evolution of religious feeling toward a more enlightened conception does not hold up to the reading of the texts. Nothing exactly corresponds to the apparition of God on Mount Sinai, to his fiery descent, to the smoke that rises "as the smoke of a furnace," to a whole mountain that "quaked greatly" (Exodus 19:18). He even orders Moses, responding to him "in thunder"[2] (Exodus 19:19), to warn the priests and the people not to cross the boundaries he has set in order to climb up toward him, "lest he break forth upon them" (Exodus 19:24). This last expression is particularly frightening, *repelling*; it puts our intelligence in its place, with its desire to understand. However, the New Testament, which constantly probes the Old, fully recognizes this terrible God. The author of the Epistle to the Hebrews exhorts

---

2   In the New American Standard Bible (NASB), this verse reads, "God answered him with thunder."

his readers to remain faithful to the God of Sinai, to him "whose voice then shook the earth" (Hebrews 12:26), while also recalling the revelation of God in Deuteronomy 4:24 and in Isaiah 33:14, "for our God is a consuming fire" (Hebrews 12:29). Meditating on other passages such as "Vengeance is mine" (Deuteronomy 32:35), the same author cries, "It is a fearful thing to fall into the hands of the living God" (Hebrews 10:31). Paul, remembering another oft-repeated expression—when Miriam and Aaron, for example, become jealous of Moses, "and the anger of the Lord was kindled against them" (Numbers 12:9)—declares, in a prose that itself is kindled, that "the wrath of God is revealed from heaven against all ungodliness and unrighteousness of men, who hold the truth in unrighteousness" (Romans 1:18). But how does this wrath reveal itself? Where do we see it? The *ungodly* and the *unrighteous* are not burned here below, apparently, by any divine fire. It is revealed in the frenzy of their ungodliness. "Wherefore God also gave them up to uncleanness through the lusts of their own hearts, to dishonor their own bodies. . . . For this cause God gave them up unto vile affections. . . . God gave them over to a reprobate mind, to do those things which are not convenient": injustice, perversity, greed, and so on (Romans 1:24–28). As Otto says, the revelation of a God who *gives sinners over* to their sins causes us to tremble with incomprehension. It reminds us of what God imposes on Pharaoh before the exodus—"I will harden his heart, that he shall not let the people go" (Exodus 4:21)—and the repetition, during successive plagues, of this divine act that disarms our idea of justice.

Then the encounters with Jesus in the Gospels often offer the alarming vision of a holiness that absolutely transcends the known and the knowable. The transfiguration is now so familiar to us— paradoxically, in part because of its numerous artistic depictions—that it seems difficult for us to feel the inordinate power of this unique moment when Jesus is actually changed by eternity into himself, when a window is opened onto heaven, when the voice of God, as in the Old Testament, resounds in a cloud.[3] According to Luke's version, Peter, John, and James contemplate the ineffable *glory*: the glory of Jesus and the glory of Moses and Elijah (Luke 9:31–32). Dazzled by the "glistering" whiteness—which now has nothing earthly about it—of Jesus's clothing and the appearance of his face, which becomes other ("altered"; Luke 9:29), they "feared as they entered into the cloud" (Luke 9:34), as in Mark's narrative (9:6) and that of Matthew (17:6), where they fall on their faces. The only moment when Jesus, a man who eats and sleeps like other men, appears in the glory of his Godhead is both exhilarating and terrible for the three disciples, and for us if we listen to its account with spiritual imagination.

And why do certain people react to Jesus in what can seem a rather excessive manner? Exactly what do they see? In Matthew's account, the centurion and the soldiers who guarded Jesus during the crucifixion, "fear[ing] greatly" in the midst of the earthquake following his death and the open tombs, exclaim, "Truly this was the Son of God!" (Matthew 27:54). According to Luke, at the very moment when Jesus breathes his last, the centurion alone glorifies God and says, "Certainly this was a righteous man!" (Luke 23:47). But here is Mark's version: "And Jesus cried with a loud voice, and gave up the ghost. And the veil of the temple was rent in twain from the top to the bottom. And when the centurion, which stood over against him, saw that he so cried out, and gave up the ghost, he said, 'Truly this man was the Son of God!'" (Mark 15:37–39). That the centurion and his soldiers should continue to be persuaded of the extraordinary stature of Jesus after the earthquake and the open graves is easily understood. But what does the centurion see

---

3   The phrase "is changed by eternity into himself" is an echo from a famous poem by Stéphane Mallarmé, *Le Tombeau d'Edgar Poe*, which all French readers would quickly recognize.

when Jesus dies facing him, according to all appearances like hundreds of others he has seen crucified? We do not know, but the reverential fear that is heard in his words leaves us to suppose that he sees a difference in Jesus, his belonging to a fearfully different divine world. And if we listen well to this pagan, we can feel the same deferential fear, as before the fact that he did not of himself understand the nature of Jesus, but that the Holy Spirit must have revealed it to him.

And Thomas? What does he see as he makes his famous confession of faith in the Gospel of John? He first refuses to believe in the resurrection unless he can touch the marks on Jesus's body, like those who will not believe in "Christianity" without documentary or logical proofs. However, does one not feel in the exaggeration of his words his sadness, his desire to believe and yet his inability fully to succeed? "Except I shall see in his hands the print of the nails and put my finger into the print of the nails and thrust my hand into his side, I will not believe" (John 20:25). We are far from the language of someone who is defining the criteria of a conviction. Jesus appears before him and reproves him very gently, inviting him to place his finger "here" in his hands and to hold out his hand to put it in his side, knowing full well that he will not do so. Immediately comes Thomas's cry: "My Lord and my God!" (John 20:28). It is the most clairvoyant confession in the entire Gospel, the only one to recognize Jesus as God. It is given to him to discern in Jesus, whose wounds he doubtless doesn't even look at, something of the fearful mystery of the Godhead, an immensity of presence that opens his spirit, astounds him, and fills him with wonder.

At the moment of his conversion, Paul encounters this same Jesus, both terrifying and tender. The Acts of the Apostles recounts how, on the road to Damascus, "there shined round about him a light from heaven," and a voice called him by name (Acts 9:3–4). He falls to the ground before this manifestation of the totally other. When he recounts the episode to King Agrippa, he describes the light as "above the brightness of the sun" (Acts 26:13), supernatural and foreign to our capacity to conceive it. To the Jews in Jerusalem, he explains that he could no longer see "for the glory of that light" (Acts 22:11). This is most certainly the fearful glory of Jesus that he saw with a heart so estranged from him that it blinds him. However, in evoking this encounter before Agrippa, Paul recalls that after telling him, "Saul, Saul, why persecutest thou me?" Jesus continues thus: "It is hard for thee to kick against the pricks" (Acts 26:14). Jesus shows him what he had refused to admit, that his fury against the Christians came from the thought, intolerable for such a zealous Jew, that they were perhaps right. But Jesus does not accuse him; the same Son of God who blinds him by his presence speaks to him with empathy, with the help of a familiar proverbial expression.

And here is the most compelling passage. To the soldiers coming to arrest "Jesus the Nazarene," Jesus replies, "I am he," or literally, "I am." At these words, writes John, "they went backward, and fell to the ground" (John 18:6). The Jerusalem Bible assumes that it is the divine name, the *I am* that is not to be pronounced, that frightens them. Is it not rather Jesus himself in the instant that he so names himself, when he suddenly *appears* as God himself, who strikes them with fear and causes them to retreat and fall? He then speaks to them in simple terms: "If therefore ye seek me, let these go their way" (John 18:8), doubtless so they can pull themselves together and events may take their course.

5.

The people who cross paths with Jesus in the Gospels do not always encounter a gentle being; they often feel fearful. The Gospel of Luke even begins by showing that all those who played a role in his advent had already been frightened. The angel of the Lord appears and announces to Zechariah the birth of John the Baptist; Zechariah "was troubled, and fear [*phobos*] fell upon him" (Luke 1:12). The angel tells him, "Fear not" (*mè phobou*; Luke 1:13). Mary is "troubled" by the angel Gabriel's greeting; seeing this, he reassures her, "Fear not" (*mè phobou*; Luke 1:29–30). At the birth of John the Baptist, "fear [*phobos*] came on all that dwelt round about them" (Luke 1:65). When the angel of the Lord descends upon the shepherds, they are "sore afraid" (*phobos*; Luke 2:9); the angel tells them, "Fear not" (*mè phobeisthe*; Luke 2:10). As with the acclamation of the celestial army already cited, which speaks of the glory of God but also of the peace that he dispenses, Luke from the outset emphasizes the intervention into our world of Another, celestial and frightening, and the goodwill that inspires it, the gentleness ("Fear not") that accompanies it—in order, I suppose, for readers to hold together in their minds what seems to us in our ignorance two opposite aspects of the divine nature.

He continues to highlight this fearful astonishment as he recounts the life of Jesus in his Gospel and that of the first Christians in the Acts of the Apostles. The witnesses are "all amazed" or "filled with fear" (the Greek word used being almost always *phobos* or the related verb) when Jesus heals a demoniac (Luke 4:36) or a paralytic (5:26), when he raises a dead man to life (7:16), when he calms the wind and seas of a lake (8:25). Same reaction to "wonders and signs" accomplished by the apostles (Acts 2:43); when Peter heals a man lame from birth (3:10); when Ananias, accused by Peter of embezzling, falls dead (5:5) and his wife Sapphira suffers the same fate (5:11); when a Roman centurion, Cornelius, has the vision of an angel (10:4); when an evil spirit attacks and wounds some itinerant exorcists claiming to be adherents of Paul (19:17). At the death of Sapphira, "great fear came upon all the church" (5:11). The fear is obviously reverential, but we should not minimize its discomfort—we should not forget that it is indeed a matter of *fear*.

Whence the importance of the first miraculous catch of fish. Simon at first refuses Jesus's advice, to go out into deep water and cast his nets, on grounds that he and his companions have labored an entire night without catching anything. Is it something in Jesus's gaze that makes him suddenly change his mind? They catch so many fish that the two boats sink. "When Simon Peter saw it, he fell down at Jesus' knees, saying, 'Depart from me, for I am a sinful man, O Lord.' For he was astonished, and all that were with him" (Luke 5:8–9). Simon's horrified reaction recalls that of Isaiah in the Old Testament. Seeing the fearful alterity of Jesus, he recognizes himself as a sinner, the way Isaiah recognizes himself as a man with unclean lips. He goes so far as to beg him to go away, so terrible is this vision of who Jesus is—or rather the ignorance of who this prodigious man could well be.

Would this be the same guilty feeling that makes the entire population of the region of the Gadarenes beg him to leave? One would not say so at first blush. Jesus heals a possessed man and sends the devils into a herd of pigs. Seeing the demoniac healed and in his right mind, the people are "afraid" (*ephobèthèsan*; Luke 8:35), and one could think they just want to get rid of him, through a sort of panic at a strange being with fearful powers who has also made them lose a goodly herd. However, at the moment when Luke announces that the crowd that has come running "besought him to depart from them; for they were taken with great fear" (*phobô megolô*; Luke 8:37), not only does he recapitulate their fear, but he uses almost the same expression—"depart from them"—as for Simon ("Depart from me"). It is possible that the Gadarenes too find in their fear the revelation of their own nature.

Whatever the case, it is evident when one reads the Gospels carefully that Jesus ceaselessly strikes fear in all kinds of circumstances.

And what could be more incomprehensible than to send the devils into pigs, who plunge from the top of an escarpment and drown in the sea? We could even conclude that the Gospel recounts the incident precisely for its total strangeness, in order to shake us, perplex us.

6.

For we too encounter in Jesus a holy being. During communion, knowing that the bread and wine are his body and his blood is enough for us to be raised into a fearful and joyous world. They in themselves alone impose a presence both salutary and other. In the prayer that Jesus taught his disciples, we enter with the very first words into the same mystery. In saying "Our Father which art in heaven," we pass from an intimacy with God into the declaration of his remoteness in *heaven*, whose meaning is hidden from us. Otto felicitously calls this harmony between two acts of consciousness a "chord of dominant seventh." And if we have the right to call God "Abba, Father" (Romans 8:15, Galatians 4:6), it is remarkable that Jesus, who like us says "Abba, Father" (Mark 14:36), also addresses him as "Holy Father" (John 17:11).

For the holiness of God constitutes the basso continuo of the New Testament as well as the Old. God reveals to everyone, regardless of their religion or irreligion, "his eternal power and Godhead" (Romans 1:20). Paul thus places him beyond our conception. If *God* (*theos*) reveals his *Godhead* (*theiotès*), he is manifesting nothing other than what he is: himself, God. By the same token, his eternal power escapes our notion of power, being other; the adjective *eternal* does not just signify *enduring forever*. And it is this God who descends into our world at the moment of the incarnation. The words of the angel Gabriel explaining to Mary how she is going to give birth, "The Holy Ghost shall come upon thee, and the power of the Highest shall overshadow thee" (Luke 1:35), recall those of

Paul. She will know in herself the eternal power and Godhead of God, exercised no doubt with an infinite gentleness. But that the Christian should be involved in this Godhead makes one tremble. In another letter, Paul, while affirming that in Jesus dwells bodily "all the fullness of the Godhead [*theotètos*]" and continuing thus— "ye are complete in him" (Colossians 2:9–10)—makes us grow pale with fear and shame. The author of the Epistle to the Hebrews also declares that God corrects us (and we could have guessed it) "for our profit," but most particularly (and we would never have found this) "that we might be partakers of his holiness" (12:10). After two thousand years of reiteration, his words demand our full attention to realize their power. If holiness belongs to God alone and names the remoteness of his Godhead, how are we to reach it? The Bible shows us the path, but must we not dig into this revelation with fear and trembling rather than accepting it for granted as a simple teaching to put into practice? Paul explains to the Ephesians, moreover, that they constitute a "holy temple" in the making (Ephesians 2:21); Peter calls Christians a "holy nation" (1 Peter 2:9). The most secret and fearful aspect of God should characterize us as well.

Finally, let us recognize that the Bible, which reveals to us the holiness of God, is also a manifestation of it. Paul presents the gospel as the promise made long ago by God "in the holy scriptures" (Romans 1:2); he reminds Timothy that he has known the "holy scriptures" (2 Timothy 3:15) since his early childhood. We should not let the familiarity of the expression "the Holy Bible" mask its strange and numinous nature from us. One must listen to all Scripture "given by inspiration of God" (2 Timothy 3:16) in silence with the hope of hearing and understanding. It is not a matter of making this object, this book, into an idol, but of respecting the absolute difference of the word it transmits.

And let us not suppose that Bible reading is second-best, words on a page remaining necessarily inert, and that the word becomes a powerful presence only when it is heard in a lived situation. Otto approvingly cites in this sense a passage from Henri Suso: "It is one thing to hear oneself the melodious chords of a lyre; another thing to hear someone speak of them. Similarly, words received in a state of grace emanating from a living heart and pronounced by a living mouth are one thing; another when the same words are inscribed on a dead scroll."[4] The analogy is false. To read the Bible with understanding, one must listen to it resonate, the way one reads a poem, but with this difference: the voice that speaks is God's, addressing each reader individually.

At bottom, Otto refuses even to listen to this word when it contradicts his presuppositions. He accuses Ezekiel of having drawn a fantasy picture of Yahweh and his court, of bowing to "the taste for the miraculous, for legend, for the world of apocalyptic and mystical dreams," of thus getting in the way of the radiance of "the pure sentiment of mystery." To decide for oneself what constitutes the sacred, to analyze it in the manner of a European intellectual, forcibly puts stoppers in one's ears. The prolific and outlandishly bizarre visions of Ezekiel afford a glimpse of the true alterity of God. Otto also believes himself superior to the writers of the New Testament. He finds that John, when he has Thomas say, "My Lord and my God" (John 20:28), bears witness to a rather late period "which aimed too far and too high and had already strayed from the simplicity of the original experience." What he says about this original simplicity is admirable. Commenting on a passage from Mark—"And they were in the way going up to Jerusalem; and Jesus went before them: and they were amazed; and as they followed, they were afraid" (Mark 10:32), where their amazement and fear probably were inspired by the simple presence of Jesus, whose back is turned—Otto judges that "the greatest art of psychological

---

4 Otto, *Idea of the Holy*, 61n.

description" could not better convey the numinous impression that was emanating from Jesus.[5] And how right he is! However, one cannot permit oneself, because of a partly stylistic preference—as opposed to Mark, he says, John makes use of a "formula"—to judge a moment of John's Gospel where the numinous nature of Jesus appears in a few words and in the most striking manner.

The power of the Bible everywhere questions our assumptions. Every opening toward the sacred challenges them.

7.

Here is the God, it seems to me, whom Christians seek to know and serve and whom they wish all might have the inexpressible joy of finding. The holiness of God constitutes the best argument against the recent tendency to dilute the proclamation of truth by seeking "dialogue." It is a good thing that Christian organizations collaborate with those of other religions and with everyone to promote the common good. It is certain that we are not to judge, for that is forbidden. However, the partisans of dialogue, after having insisted for a moment on the supreme truth of the gospel, return to what seems to them of equal importance: mutual understanding and tolerance, which are necessary but not sufficient. Such an approach can seem generous, open, when insisting on the unique nature of Christianity, maintaining on the subject of Jesus that "there is none other name under heaven given among men, whereby we must be saved" (Acts 4:12), points, for many, to pride and sectarianism. But where does the mission for dialogue come from? From the evolution of society? From our guilty conscience? From an influx of good feelings? Surely not from the Bible. After his resurrection, Jesus does not send his disciples into the world to study other religions and

---

5 Otto, 61n.

find what they have in common with them. He tells them in the Gospel of Matthew, "All power is given unto me in heaven and in earth. Go ye therefore and teach all nations" (Matthew 28:19). In Mark, "Go ye into all the world, and preach the gospel to every creature. He that believeth and is baptized shall be saved; but he that believeth not shall be damned" (Mark 16:15–16). In Luke, "Thus it is written, and thus it behoved Christ to suffer, and to rise from the dead the third day, and that repentance and remission of sins should be preached in his name among all nations" (Luke 24:46–47). All Christians know these texts. Why not listen to them? To know how to bring the good news to adherents of other religions, why not study Paul's discourse at the Areopagus in Athens (Acts 17)? For Jews, before whom a Christian is certainly nothing more than a wild olive branch grafted onto the mother plant (Romans 11:24), why not study Paul's preaching in the synagogue at Antioch (Acts 13)? The woolliness of dialogue neglects the holy sovereignty of Christ.

The Bible orders Christians to love others—each of them—not primarily to facilitate getting along with them or world peace. To love one's neighbors is to wish them the greatest good, which is to know Jesus. Focusing on dialogue is a failure to love.

Love indeed, and if I have concentrated in this chapter on the holiness of God, I have not forgotten that the God who seeks us and who sent his Son to die in our place is love, goodness, and mercy. If the word of salvation must be "in demonstration of the Spirit and of power" (1 Corinthians 2:4), it can be so by presenting at the same time, and in a unity without paradox whatsoever, the alterity of the God of justice and the humility of the God who gives himself to us. It presents the death and resurrection of a Jesus who simply asks us to come while reminding us that this Savior of an unfathomable kindness is at the same time "the Lord of glory" (1 Corinthians 2:8), the "brightness" of God's "glory," the one who "uphold[s] all things by the word of his power" (Hebrews 1:3).

The gospel provokes, by the force of its proclamation, not shame but a feeling of guilt. Through shame one realizes that one has not measured up to the image one has built of oneself. One confesses, in short, to oneself, one's superego. Shame is painful but is not accompanied by awe. Guilt places us in front of the other and, when the sentiment is generalized (what one does or doesn't do is no longer in question; it is what one is), before the Other, before God. Such is the situation of Peter's audience at Pentecost, who are "pricked in their heart" and ask, "What shall we do?" (Acts 2:37). Shame makes us withdraw within ourselves; guilt makes us repent. Here we find once again the very beginning of Jesus's preaching: "Repent: for the kingdom of heaven is at hand" (Matthew 4:17).

We also perhaps discover the explanation for a passage of Psalm 51 that is, on first reading, shocking: "Against thee, thee only, have I sinned." It is to be assumed that in this famous poem, David is asking forgiveness for having slept with Bathsheba and plotted the death of her husband. An adulterer and murderer, how can he pretend that his sin concerns only God, without thinking of his victims and even excluding them from his confession? Does he understand—but this is only speculation—that he must concentrate all his attention on the God he has offended in order for the horror of his actions to appear and, above all, the horror of what he is? Hence this plunge into the abyss of the soul: "Behold, I was shapen in iniquity; and in sin did my mother conceive me" (Psalm 51:5). I believe the Jerusalem Bible is wrong to affirm in a note that this fundamental impurity is alleged as an extenuating circumstance. The seriousness of his confession allows David to see the deep rootedness of evil in the fall, to discern that the sin already within him has made him commit grave offenses.

His guilt seizes him in the presence of the God who is pure, holy, and other. But also before the God of love and mercy, for the Psalm begins thus: "Have mercy upon me, O God, according to thy lovingkindness: according unto the multitude of thy tender mercies blot out my transgressions." David contemplates at a single glance both the totally other Godhead of God and the love through which he abases himself to our level, fallen but made in his image.

2

Faith Is Knowing

1.

Faith is the discovery of the real, the moment of our awakening, of putting ourselves in a relationship with the holy God and with a world transformed by a new gaze. A certain philosophy, as well as the man on the street, distinguishes clearly between believing and knowing. *I know that such and such a proposition is true* means both that I am certain of it and that this certainty is founded on material or logical proofs. *I believe it* presupposes an absence of certainty and decisive proofs. In the second case, if I acknowledge that I am not sure of what I am asserting, no one doubts my honesty or the level of my intelligence. Up to that point, everything is fine, everyone agrees. Things take a turn for the worse as soon as it is a matter of Christian faith, where those who say *I believe—I believe in God, I believe the Bible, I believe Jesus rose from the dead*—are asked for proofs, and when their questioners do not receive them, they impute in them a deplorable weak-mindedness. People concede that there is a, let us say, subjective difference between such affirmations and, for example, *I believe that Erasmus was born in Rotterdam*, but they will not stop insisting that the objective criteria we ordinarily require must also validate or invalidate the propositions undergirding these Christian affirmations: *God exists*; *the Bible is the word of God*; *Jesus rose from the dead*. And Christians reinforce the confusion—for confusion there is—by speaking, precisely, of propositions, of dogmas, whereas faith, at bottom, is not just adhering to a set of beliefs but rather a particular form of knowing. Faith, foreign to our ways of being and thinking, is *something else altogether*.

It is distinguished from credulity and intellectual assent because it is a secure knowledge—or rather, a *secure knowing*. The verb translates better than the noun the active nature of faith, just as, properly considered, *being acquainted with* would suggest better than *knowing* its transitiveness. The Christian does not believe, primarily, that certain things are true. He believes God; he knows Jesus. Faith is neither the outcome of a thought nor, for that matter, the fruit of an emotion nor the accomplishment of a desire nor a leap into the void. The English language allows us to express its reality with exactness: faith is less a *knowledge* than a *knowing*, the entering into a relationship with something or someone. Two passages of the New Testament make believing and knowing coincide. When Jesus asks the Twelve if they want to leave as others have just done, Peter—after saying decidedly not, for Jesus has the words of eternal life—adds, "We believe and are sure [or literally, we have believed and known] that thou art that Christ, the Son of the living God" (John 6:69). Is he separating the action of believing (*pepisteukamen*) from that of knowing (*egnôkamen*)? Or is he rather reinforcing his faith and that of his friends by calling it "knowing"? James, speaking to a hypothetical Christian who is persuaded that faith can do without works says sarcastically, "Thou believest [*pisteueis*] that there is one God;

thou doest well: the devils also believe" (*pisteuousi*; James 2:19). The simple fact of believing in the existence of one and only one God is not true faith; it does not save men any more than it saves demons.

Seen from the outside, Christianity presents itself, nonetheless, partly through the fault of Christians, as a belief system at first blush incredible and for which the discovery of rational proof seems more than doubtful. Considering things from the outside in *The Future of an Illusion*, Freud sees the Christian God—unique and paternal—as a culmination of comforting ancestral beliefs: providence watches over us, a moral order governs the universe, death ushers us into a new existence. In his *Philosophical Investigations*, Wittgenstein imagines that "religion teaches that the soul can subsist when the body has decomposed," and he reflects on this possibility. This is not exactly what Christianity teaches, and once again, to examine doctrines as one would examine theses of structural anthropology or arguments in favor of expanding European unification is to put the cart before the horse, beliefs before faith. André Gide approves "non-acquiescence to dogmas" in the name of integrity of the mind, of human dignity, of a moral life that refuses "the support and comfort of Faith." The Christian does not recognize himself in acquiescing to dogma nor in reducing faith to comfort. This passage from one of Gide's *Imaginary Interviews* is cited in *Can One Choose Not to Believe?* by Jacques Bouveresse, who in a similar vein refers to the necessity of rigor, logic, and self-respect that can "prevent one from believing." But why does a Christian believe, for example, in eternal life? It is thanks to his experience of Christ, of a person (if the word is fitting) who transcends our world of birth and death, and because the faith that he has received allows him to discern the authority with which the Bible speaks of the resurrection of the dead. If he believed in eternal life only as a church teaching or as one of the doctrines of a religion called Christianity, he could very well lose that belief under the pressure of a critical examination, and perhaps intellectual integrity would require such renunciation. Have those who think they have "lost their faith" not rather lost their belief and a set of beliefs? Does not all this take place on the secular level, as, for example, with someone who used to be a sincere socialist, convinced of the truth of socialist principles, but no longer is?

It is, in a sense, unreasonable to ask a God who has already revealed himself to provide proof. We often behave as Pharisees of intellectual rectitude, standing firm on our wisdom and regarding with a severe eye a God who is offering himself to us. Yet if faith is a gift of God, so is reason—on another level, not that of salvation but of the creation—just as the search for proof, the ardor of argument, and the pleasure of being sure. By holding that faith is *other* are we asking the intellect to make "sacrifices" (Bouveresse)? In the absence of verification or falsification, even of elementary rules of logic, just how may faith be considered a knowing?

2.

Take a few examples from the Gospels. The Synoptic Gospels tell the story of a woman who, having suffered from a hemorrhage for twelve years, approaches Jesus from behind and touches the hem of his garment: "For she said within herself, 'If I may but touch his garment, I shall be whole'" (Matthew 9:21; Mark 5:28). "I shall be whole" (*sôthèsomai*): doesn't the future tense of the verb convey more than a simple confidence? The woman *knows* she will be whole, and she is right. Mark and Luke state precisely that the healing took place as soon as she touched the garment, and Jesus confirms this by a sentence that resonates repeatedly in the Synoptic Gospels: "Thy faith hath made thee whole" (Matthew 9:22; Mark 5:34; Luke 8:48). Faith here *is* knowing, and it is up to us to wonder how this anonymous woman has arrived at that certainty and what that certainty consists of psychologically. And what we are considering here is indeed the faith that saves. Since the verb *sôzein* means both "heal" and "save," both meanings are to be construed each time Jesus pronounces the words "Hè pistis sou sesôke se" (Thy faith hath saved thee). The Jerusalem Bible always renders it "saved you," which could seem at first sight an exaggeration, the deletion of an everyday medical term in favor of a religious concept. Do not nearly all the people Jesus addresses in this way simply wish him to heal an infirmity? However, another narrative, this one about ten lepers, reveals the deeper dimension of the word, latent in all these stories. They ask Jesus to have pity on them, and they are cleansed. They go off to show themselves to the priests, and only one turns around in his tracks and falls prostrate at Jesus's feet to thank him. "Arise, go thy way, thy faith hath made thee whole," says Jesus (Luke 17:19)— *saved* is the meaning here, for he is already healed. Must we think that the nine other lepers only wanted to benefit from the powers of an exceptional man whose healings had been noised about, whereas the tenth—a Samaritan—was the only one who had faith?

One might say that the illnesses healed by Jesus represent a more radical flaw, the sin that he also erases, the entirety of our fallen condition that he came to remedy. The word *heal/save* has in all these cases the same unfathomable meaning as earlier in the Gospel of Luke, when Jesus says of the devil that he steals away from some the sown seed of the word, "lest they should believe and be saved" (*sôthôsin*; 8:12), or later, when he proclaims that he has come "to seek and to save [*sôsai*] that which was lost" (19:10). Let us also note that the leper and the woman afflicted with a flow of blood, like the others saved by their faith, are seeking personal benefit. Their faith is neither a disinterested contemplation of Jesus nor the result of objective reasoning. They are seeking a benefit, Jesus grants it, and he does not refuse to give to their desire, to their expectation, the name of faith.

I open a parenthesis in this series of examples in order to bring
in purely human knowing in its encounter with miracles. Jairus, the
ruler of the synagogue who comes begging Jesus to heal his dying
daughter, is told by a messenger that his daughter has already died.
When he arrives at the home, Jesus declares that she is not dead, only
sleeping. The crowd laughs him to scorn, "knowing that she [is] dead"
(Luke 8:53). This knowing is quite correct, the laughing crowd are
not mistaken, his daughter is actually dead, no doubt—except for
Jesus, who knows that he will raise her to life, and, it seems, Jairus,
who says to Jesus in Matthew's version, "My daughter is even now
dead, but come and lay thy hand on her and she shall live" (Matthew
9:18). "She shall live": the future tense of the verb bears testimony,
here again, to another knowing, to a faith that knows.

Next take the story of the two blind men in Matthew 9:27–31.
Like the lepers, they beg Jesus to have pity on them, but this time
Jesus asks them, "Believe ye that I am able to do this?" They answer
"yes"; he touches their eyes, saying, "According to your faith be
it unto you"; and their eyes are opened. He does not ask them
whether, all things considered, weighing the pros and cons, and
sifting through the rumors about him, they believe him capable
of healing them. Neither does he require their acquiescence to the
proposition "Jesus can heal sicknesses." Their "yes" is the affirma-
tion of those who know, and the healing of their eyes, according
to their faith, is proof of it. Once again, they are not disinterested,
and, like all those who acknowledge their need to be healed, they
do not trouble themselves over the morality of assent, of knowing
they have the right to know. They find themselves in Jesus's pres-
ence; they believe in him. In Jesus's absence, and after his death
and resurrection, we are not asked to do otherwise: "I determined
not to know anything among you," writes Paul to the Corinthians,
"save Jesus Christ, and him crucified" (1 Corinthians 2:2). Jesus
continues to ask, fundamentally, "Do you believe I can heal you?"

Another perspective is furnished by the story of the "sinner" who washes Jesus's feet with her tears. By contrast with the other stories, here it is a matter of faith such as we recognize it. We may suppose that she is repenting of her wayward life and that she comes to Jesus knowing that he can forgive her and sensing perhaps that he, a just and good person, is the one whom she has offended above all. Jesus reacts by telling her what he does not tell the other people who have come to be healed: "Thy sins are forgiven" (Luke 7:48). Curiously, in this intimate and private story, she does not speak, and it is not a question of what she *believes*. Yet Jesus declares to her, "Thy faith hath saved thee" (*hè pistis sou sesôke se*; Luke 7:50). The verb certainly means *saved* rather than *healed*, and Jesus explains (to a Pharisee) why he has forgiven her sins: "for she loved much" (Luke 7:47). Equally unexpected is the fact that she asks for nothing; she is only seeking a personal relationship with Jesus. She knows she must go to him, she loves him almost with no ulterior motive, and Jesus calls this faith. It is neither intelligence, nor emotions, but her whole person that believes, and that believes in another person. To contemplate this extraordinary woman, (probably) a prostitute and wise, is to contemplate faith: a movement, an impulse of the soul.

Or take the story, in the Gospel of John, of the nobleman who asks Jesus to go from Cana to Capernaum to heal his dying son. Jesus tests him, it seems, by rebuffing him: "Except ye see signs and wonders, ye will not believe" (John 4:48). Instead of wasting time trying to assure Jesus that, on the contrary, he does not require proof before believing him, the nobleman repeats his prayer, doubtless with still more insistence: "Sir, come down ere my child die." He thus shows his faith, and Jesus immediately answers, "Go thy way, thy son liveth." John adds, "And the man believed the word that Jesus had spoken unto him, and he went his way" (John 4:50). He believes Jesus; he believes in the performative, efficacious word of the one whom John identifies as the creative Word of God. Why then does he ask his servants who meet him on the way the exact hour when his son began to feel better? Doubtless in order to marvel at the precision of the miracle. Learning that the fever had left him at the very hour when Jesus spoke, he "himself believed," writes John, "and his whole house" (John 4:53). It is not a case of verification nor of simple credulity in the face of a coincidence.

Last example: the centurion who, wanting Jesus to heal his young slave but not considering himself "worthy" for Jesus to enter under his roof, asks him to "speak the word only" (Matthew 8:8; Luke 7:7). The nobleman, hearing a word from Jesus, believes; the centurion goes further, for he believes in Jesus's word absolutely. Knowing the power of his own words over his soldiers and slave, he seems to recognize in Jesus, along with the authority of his person, the supernatural power of his words. Jesus himself "marvels" at this exceptional faith (Matthew 8:10; Luke 7:9). Just as to the two blind men, he says to the centurion, "As thou hast believed, so be it done unto thee" (Matthew 8:13), and the slave's healing demonstrates that the centurion's faith is a certainty, a knowing.

How do all these characters, healed or saved by faith, or whose faith assures the healing of another, know that Jesus is the source of salvation? Insofar as their certainty is a subjective experience, the question is vain. As philosopher A. J. Ayer writes in *The Problem of Knowledge*, it would be "absurd to ask someone how he knows he is suffering or how he knows that what he sees seems to have such and such a color." The woman preparing to touch Jesus's garment knows that in so doing, she will be healed; the nobleman knows that Jesus's word has just healed his son, who, however, is in another town, and the only way we can know what this knowing was is to find it in ourselves. The knowing of all those we have observed, like that of someone who looks at a green or blue object, also has an objective dimension, the very person of Jesus. Here again philosophy seems to be impotent. Since Jesus is not a proposition concerning the real, susceptible to being verified or not, if they were asked what their knowing is based on, what would they answer if not that something in Jesus struck them and that they cannot think otherwise?

Which brings us to a biblical teaching that we know well: faith is a gift of God, but we easily forget whenever we wish to consider the reasons, the arguments that lead man to faith. All these people are examples of a fundamental faith in Jesus, in his word, of an encounter with the Savior that does without reasons and even doctrines. Their faith shows perfectly what faith *is*, and we should remember them when reflecting on what they did not know about, the propitiatory death and resurrection of Jesus; on the way these events enter into our own faith; and on the way we should speak of them.

3.

Does their faith, however, really have the status of fully Christian faith? And is their salvation that which is described in the Acts of the Apostles and in the epistles of the New Testament? They did not believe, and for good reason, in half the affirmations of our credos, and they did not know that salvation depends on the sacrifice of Jesus. The answer to the two questions is certainly yes, but this *yes* stimulates further thought. For the very example of the faith that saves—Abraham—also was ignorant of nearly everything we believe. The verse of Genesis that Paul cites (Romans 4:3) in order to establish the primacy of salvation by faith over the supposed salvation by works of the Law—Abraham "believed in the Lord; and he counted it to him for righteousness" (Genesis 15:6)—simply says he had confidence in God, that he believed what God was saying. As we know, taking God's word on trust (according to the first occurrence of the word *believe* in the Bible) was not at all evident for

Abraham. God declares to him that his posterity will be as numer-
ous as the stars in the sky, though he and his wife are too old to have
children. God does not ask him to believe in his existence, but to
believe the apparently unrealizable promise he makes to him. Abra-
ham's faith, trusting in God, is thus *knowing* that his posterity will
be innumerable. It is Paul who affirms it: Abraham gave glory to
God, "fully persuaded [*plèrophorètheis*] that, what he had promised,
he was able also to perform" (Romans 4:21). Abraham illustrates
perfectly the initial definition of faith according to the author of
the Letter to the Hebrews: "Now faith is the substance of things
hoped for" (Hebrews 11:1). For in the course of his own exposition
on faith, Paul presents Abraham thus: he "against hope believed in
hope" (Romans 4:18). In spite of the evidence, he knew.

It would seem that faith is simple, of a simplicity that shocks us
if we expect God to propose a faith whose nature might exercise our
intelligence and satisfy our desire for complexity. When God says,
through the intermediary of the Bible or of a Christian, that Jesus
died and rose again for the remission of sin, it is sufficient to believe
this by a faith that is at the same time an opening of our being and a
gift of God. From that moment on, one *knows* the essential things:
that God speaks to us and loves us.

Whence the importance, at the beginning of Paul's first letter
to the Corinthians, of the strong idea that human wisdom is fool-
ishness and the foolishness of God, wisdom—an idea or, rather,
a revelation, whose consequences we have not properly measured.
Since the world, writes Paul, "by wisdom knew not God, it pleased
God by the foolishness of preaching to save them that believe"
(1 Corinthians 1:21). He was thinking of the sages among the
Greeks, philosophers and orators; we could quote, among our own
sages, Renan: "To leave the religious idea in its most complete
indetermination, to hold at the same time these two propositions:
(1) 'Religion will be eternal in humanity;' (2) 'all religious symbols

are vulnerable to attack and perishable,' such would be . . . if the *sages' sentiment* could be that of the masses, the true theology of our time" (*Philosophical Dialogues and Fragments*—my emphasis). One can imagine Paul's impatience if he read this and the pertinence of his commentary. And just what exactly does his rejection of wisdom and embrace of foolishness mean? Christ has sent me, he writes, "to preach the gospel: not with wisdom of words, lest the cross of Christ should be made of none effect" (1 Corinthians 1:17). No argument, however well structured, however compelling it might be, can lead us to the work of Christ on the cross, since the cross is "foolishness" (1:23), is set apart, is *something other*, is the "wisdom of God" (1:24): "For I determined not to know anything among you, save Jesus Christ, and him crucified. . . . And my speech and my preaching was not with enticing words of man's wisdom, but in demonstration of the Spirit and of power: that your faith should not stand in the wisdom of men, but in the power of God" (2:2–5). Like the cross, faith runs a very grave risk. A faith resting on human wisdom would be a simple intellectual belief, the assent to persuasive argument. True faith depends very precisely on the power of God; it comes from beyond, like all gifts.

This extraordinary affirmation by Paul jars us into deeper reflection. It challenges our philosophy—"The Greeks seek after wisdom, but we preach Christ crucified . . . unto the Greeks foolishness" (1 Corinthians 1:22–23)—but who is listening? We wish at all costs to defend human wisdom, the domain of intellectual belief, and when thinkers demand proof, reasons, we try to furnish them. We proclaim the rationality of faith instead of responding with Paul that we have nothing to offer but the foolishness of a message, a crucified Christ, knowing that otherwise we are reducing the work of the cross to nothing—that faith is an *other* knowing and a world of knowing to which it alone provides access.

The Christian can also invite the "disputer of this world" (1 Corinthians 1:20) to ask himself whether reason is really the master of truth and whether a religion that affirms itself as having been revealed does not require an approach that is foreign to our ways of thinking.

Do Paul's famous but neglected oxymorons—a foolish wisdom, a wise foolishness—concern only appearance? In a sense, yes. Human wisdom is foolishness *for* God, a crucified Christ is foolishness *for* pagans, but the wisdom of God *for* "them which are called" (1 Corinthians 1:24). To stop there, however, to suppose that human wisdom is not actually foolish nor the cross actually foolishness, would that not be to rob this vision of an upside-down world of its power? Human wisdom is wise insofar as one applies it to the domains for which it is relevant; it becomes really foolish when it ventures into what is beyond it. God's wisdom is infinitely and inconceivably wise; it is really foolishness for those who come up against it. We are marked out for foolishness, either human or divine, and if it is divine foolishness that welcomes us, we learn to what degree the wisdom of this foolishness is novel and unforeseeable. Addressing the Corinthians—"If any man among you seemeth to be wise in this world, let him become a fool, that he may be wise" (1 Corinthians 3:18)—Paul seems to warn Christians that worldly wisdom is always stalking us and that true wisdom awaits us when we consent to rid ourselves of worldly wisdom and become ignorant, poor, open to divine foolishness. He puts the "intellectuals" in their place by pointing out that among Christians, there are not "many wise men after the flesh"—as there are not many powerful, wellborn—but "God hath chosen the foolish things of the world to confound the wise" (1 Corinthians 1:26–27). Why do we forget that the great majority of Christians have found faith in believing quite simply in the Christ dead and risen, without passing through any rational preparation?

"Do not be surprised to see simple people believe without reasoning," writes Pascal (*Pensées*, no. 360). Indeed, why should we be surprised?

4.

By faith in a certain foolishness, one passes over a threshold, one penetrates into another world, one enjoys another knowing. In the blazing praise of faith and of the great heroes of faith that comprise the eleventh chapter of the Epistle to the Hebrews, the author is interested above all in this knowing. And if he begins this way— "Now faith is . . ." (*esti pistis* . . .)—he is concerned above all in illustrating his definition by concrete examples. His approach is narrative and existential in order that faith, described with care, might not be perceived as an idea to contemplate but a knowing in action. What could be clearer indeed than the first verse: "Now faith is the substance of things hoped for, the evidence of things not seen" (Hebrews 11:1)? "Substance" (*hypostasis*), "evidence" (*elegchos*)—the words are eloquent. Faith is situated beyond assent. *Hypostasis* signifies both the assurance that one feels and, drawing on the objective meaning it takes on in other contexts, the very substance of what one is waiting for. The French Jerusalem Bible boldly translates *hypostasis* as "guarantee" and *elegchos* as "proof." In the first chapter of the same letter, the Son of God is presented as the express image of God's person or substance (*hypostaseôs*; Hebrews 1:3). By true faith, one is assured of the benefits one hopes for, since faith itself—clarity is not without profundity—is in some way included in those benefits. Then if faith is a "guarantee," according to the skillful translation of the Jerusalem Bible, it does not need proof, being itself the "proof" of what one does not see. The word is strong—the clarity becomes a little dazzling— for it assumes that, by the faith that is given us, we experience these invisible phenomena—God, Jesus, heaven—as realities, presences.

And all this is oriented toward the future, according to the essentially practical design of the author, by the fact that these things that "we hope for" and "we do not see" inspire us to run after their attainment. The examples of faith that follow show this. Two in particular illustrate in an interesting way the action of faith as knowing. "By faith," says the author, Abraham offered Isaac as a sacrifice, knowing that his posterity depended on that only son, but judging that God had the power to "raise him up, even from the dead" (Hebrews 11:19). On first reading, this is surprising, for the thought that God could raise Isaac does not figure in the account in Genesis 22:1–14. Reflecting on the question, the author of Hebrews must have received this clarification as both an intuition and a revelation—he also illumines, by a new perspective, the stories of Abel (Hebrews 11:4) and Sara (Hebrews 11:11). It is by faith that Abraham is ready to sacrifice his son because his faith is the "substance of things hoped for"—in his case an innumerable posterity—and it gives him the understanding that to this end God is capable of overcoming death. "By faith," the author also writes, Moses left Egypt without fearing the king's fury, holding firm "as seeing him who is invisible" (Hebrews 11:27). *Ton . . . aoraton hôs horôn*: the quasi-oxymoron translates the power and the strangeness, the alterity of faith, which, as the "evidence of things not seen," renders visible, in its own way, what we, however, are incapable of seeing.

Faith is the knowledge of what does not appear. It also constitutes a knowing concerning the world that surrounds us. Already in verse 3, "Through faith we understand that the worlds were framed by the word of God, so that things which are seen were not made of things which do appear" (Hebrews 11:3). "Through faith we understand" (*pistei nooumen*): faith is presented once again as the dwelling place of another way of knowing, of an *abnormal* knowing that transcends the normal mode of knowing that is accessible by habitual ways. And must one not take into account another meaning of *nooumen*? If we *understand* that the universe was formed by God, then we *see* this too. Through the intelligence of faith, our eyes perceive *something else* in the material universe. It is once again a matter of discerning the invisible, the work of God in his creation, and our body participates in this discerning. Our incarnation in a perceptible world is not abandoned in favor of the apprehension of an idea.

This faith that understands and sees is not opposed to the *normal* study of the world, of the universe, that we call science. Through the tools at its disposal, science succeeds in grasping, always in a provisional fashion, how the reality found within our reach functions and how it could be modified. All other questions elude it. Faith goes beyond; it grasps what science as such is incapable of grasping, for it transcends a purely physical, chemical, biological, mathematical notion of the real, however complex and glowing and ingenious such a notion might be. Faith encompasses science and only contests it when it presumes to speak, in the ideological extension of its discoveries, of what it does not know. To understand that God formed the universe does not entail a literal interpretation of the beginning of Genesis and does not constitute an idea added to our experience of the world. The Christian does not perceive the world as it appears to others while telling himself from time to time and as a simple doctrine that this world is the creation of God. He *sees* differently; everything changes; God is here, absent-present in the least phenomenon.

Faith is a sudden and perpetual gift, a strange knowing. It has nothing in common with vague assurance, as in the following: "Believing where we cannot prove." I quote *In Memoriam*, a famous, melancholy poem by the English poet Tennyson, published in 1850. Through faith indeed we believe in what we cannot prove, but not as a makeshift, not in a disoriented, worried manner. True faith has no need for proof. And again: "There lives more faith in honest doubt, / Believe me, than in half the creeds." Honest doubt is certainly preferable to belief through habit or social pressure, to merely intellectual assent to propositions of the creeds, since one cannot go beyond it. In other domains, it liberates and motivates, as Michel Deguy writes in *A Man of Little Faith*: "Doubt is the exercise of the intelligence, oxygen for the work of truth. The suspension of belief is the beginning of wisdom, and all truth, being provisional, rises as a wave on an ocean of questioning."[1] But doubt does not belong to faith, cannot intervene except as an aberrant transition. Another verse from *In Memoriam* sums up what we can only call Tennyson's confusion: "We have but faith: we cannot know."

And here, finally, is the most extreme and enigmatic example of faith, offered by Jesus: "If ye have faith, and doubt not, ye shall not only do this which is done to the fig tree [cause it to wither], but also if ye shall say unto this mountain, 'Be thou removed, and be thou cast into the sea'; it shall be done" (Matthew 21:21). It would never occur to us to want to cast a mountain into the sea. Jesus is spurring us, it seems, by hyperbole, to reflect on the infinite power of God, which could be exercised through our faith, if this were up to the level of our calling, and to reflect as well on the nature of such a faith and on the way we would experience it. The corresponding passage in the Gospel of Mark emphasizes a particularly surprising aspect of this affirmation: "Have faith in God. For verily I say unto you, that whosoever shall say unto this mountain, 'Be thou removed, and be thou cast into the sea;' and shall not doubt in his heart, but shall believe that those things which he saith shall come to pass; he shall have whatsoever he saith" (Mark 11:22–23). "Those things which he saith shall come to pass": Jesus seems to promise that the language of him who believes and does not doubt will

---

1   Michel Deguy, *A Man of Little Faith* (Albany: SUNY Press, 2014).

be performative, that human language will operate (at an infinitely lower remove), like God's: "Let there be light. . . . Be thou removed and be thou cast into the sea." But how does one pass from doubt to faith? Certainly, this is not a psychological process, an intense effort of auto-suggestion, as if, by a formidable concentration of the will, one would manage finally to believe that the impossible displacement of a mountain is possible. Jesus precisely states the only condition of this apparently unlimited power: "Have faith in God." This assumes, above all, an intimate relationship with him and a submission to his will ("Thy will be done") rather than one's own. In order to move a mountain, one would have to be convinced that God wills it to move, and God alone can give this conviction, God alone can remove doubt and replace it with the faith that knows. If in hypothetical and improbable circumstances, one knew by faith that God desired, by our intervention and by the sound of our words, the transporting of a mountain, the mountain would move.

Faith is a gift; faith is a knowing. And this reasoning has a fully practical importance, far from the hardly imaginable case of a moving mountain, for Jesus adds this: "And all things, whatsoever ye shall ask in prayer, believing, ye shall receive" (Matthew 21:22); "What things soever ye desire, when ye pray, believe that ye receive them, and ye shall have them" (Mark 11:24). And yet Christians pray for the sick who are not healed; they pray to be preserved from war and war breaks out. Paul says he has prayed three times in vain for a "thorn in the flesh" to be removed; at an entirely different level, Jesus asks three times for the Father to spare him the cross, without that being granted. However, Jesus knows, at the same time, that his will must yield to the Father's, and Paul understands finally that Christ, desiring his power to be displayed in the apostle's weakness, is refusing his request. One must always pray with fervor, but it is only when we know, by the faith given us, that such is the will of God that the miraculous occurs.

That faith is a knowing does not render it any less a confidence, a marveling gaze upon God, an engagement regarding Jesus. Everything is in this relationship. The Bible is a continuous questioning of the reader and a prodigious expansion of reality. It is even to be supposed that its definition eludes us, that as soon as we stray from the very words that present it in the Bible, we become lost in our own wisdom.

Faith above all, and all the rest is vague assurance.[2] But not really above *all*, for, as Paul writes, "And though I have all faith, so that I could remove mountains, and have not charity, I am nothing" (1 Corinthians 13:2). To love God and love one's neighbor is the invitation to a whole other depth of knowing, of knowledge, of relationship.

2　Once again, Edwards quotes a very well-known line of French poetry, this time Paul Verlaine's *Art poétique*: "De la musique avant toute chose! . . . et tout le reste est littérature" (Music above all else . . . and all the rest is [but] literature).

3

On Joy

1.

The Christian's experience, and that of Christians among themselves, would also change if we rejected certain trends of thought and certain practices that privilege either a morose Christianity fleeing the "nothingness" of earthly life or, on the other hand, a sentimental, exuberant Christianity that may well be superficial. The Bible draws our attention to an astounding joy.

Is it improper to speak of joy? Cruel, when the world is suffering? No, as long as we proceed with fear and trembling and discern in joy something other than an agreeable emotion. As long as we feel that joy, far from isolating us in our well-being, opens us to others and to the real, and that, properly mysterious, it carries within it a salutary exhortation, something eminently desirable and perhaps, we will see, always to be desired.

Joy is not happiness; it transcends it. For life, and for under-
standing life, it turns out to be far more important. Certain philos-
ophers, among them Bergson and Spinoza, went so far as to think
that joy is intimately connected with the deepest intention of life.
For Bergson, in *Mind Energy*, joy "always proclaims that life has
succeeded, that it has made ground, that it has gained a victory:
all great joy has a triumphal note."[1] For Spinoza, in the fourth part
of *Ethics*, joy is the condition of one who "acts well" in confor-
mity with "things such as they are in themselves," recognizing that
"everything follows from the necessity of the divine nature, and
occurs according to the laws and eternal rules of nature."[2] To be
joyful would be to maintain oneself in the heart of the surge of life,
in the heart of an immense All.

Joy would be an imperative issuing from reality; we would be
obligated to seek it. True joy is other and much more than the joy
we ordinarily conceive and feel. Literature and all forms of art offer
us reflections of it. Whatever the subject of the work—so often
distressing, terrible, sad—the material of the work, words, sounds,
lines, colors, volumes, movements, seems to transcend it. The joy of
form is *undeniable*; it takes hold of us as soon as we direct our atten-
tion to it. It transcends the simple Aristotelian pleasure of good
imitation, of the success with which something, even unpleasant,
like the hanging carcass of an ox or King Lear's madness, is repre-
sented. It constitutes a kind of *excess* of the work, which is situated,
however, in the heart of the work, as if the goal of art were to create
a joy that is often paradoxical, always independent and sui generis.
Think of the joy in the music of Schubert's *Death and the Maiden*;
in the painting of, precisely, Rembrandt's *Slaughtered Ox*; in the
language, the narrative, the sense of the fable in Shakespeare's *King*

---

1   Henri Bergson, *Mind Energy: Lectures and Essays*, trans. H. Wildon Carr (London: Palgrave Mac-
    Millan, 2007).
2   Benedict de [Baruch] Spinoza, *Ethics*, trans. Edwin Curley (London: Penguin, 1996).

Lear. At the very moment when the work stirs our compassion, fear, indignation, deep sorrow, a great joy surprises us. It must doubtless be called an aesthetic joy, but it is not a simple joy of the aesthete, a delight that fails to concern the whole person and that excludes the consciousness of reality. Perhaps the intuition of a beauty that contradicts life's misery and allows us to glimpse something beyond the misery.

Literature can show us this particular joy and lead us to grasp it with precision. In Shakespeare's *The Tempest*, the characters find themselves on an imaginary, almost deserted, island, assembled by Prospero's magic. At the end, Prospero regains the duchy of which he had been despoiled, his daughter is engaged to a king's son, those who were thought dead are alive, those who had been taken captive by a terrifying spell and thought to have been shipwrecked discover that they are safe and sound. We could have judged this ending too easy. But the audience easily sees that it is not simply a matter of a *happy ending*. One of the characters, commenting on the situation that is suddenly revealed to them, thus exhorts the others to welcome it: "O, rejoice / Beyond a common joy."[3] An excess of joy, an excessive joy is appropriate for them because everything is happening under the sign of wonderment—in a famous line Miranda marvels before the "brave new world"[4]—and behind the magic of Prospero is profiled the action of the gods, who have "chalked forth the way" leading to this dénouement.[5] His magic is the glimpse of a true miracle. The audience as well as the characters pass "beyond a common joy," cross a threshold, encounter a new world where the divine reigns.

Whence, perhaps, the partly hidden meaning of the title of the play. If the characters come to know, with a tempest at sea that is

---

3 5.1.206–7. References are to act, scene, and line.
4 5.1.183.
5 5.1.203.

in reality an illusion, a violent spiritual and psychological upheaval that is quite real, do they not also benefit from the meaning of the Latin word behind *tempest*: *tempestus*, "coming at the right time"? Their singular joy is produced by that kind of providence that unites them at the right moment and the right place for the supernatural to be unveiled to them and for them to rejoice in seeing the apparently impossible materialize. Whence also the secret reason Prospero finally renounces magic and Shakespeare renounces his art. The writer understands that he can do anything in fiction, where nothing resists him; that he can resolve, by the magic of imagination, all the problems of a dramatic situation and stir up among his characters an overflow of joy and the exhilarating feeling of having entered a renewed world. But he also knows that, in reality, the glimpse of the miraculous and the extreme joy that accompanies it is a gift—a gift of the real, a gift of the gods—and that his art here is discovering its limits. The greatness of *The Tempest*, its importance in theater, comes from this clear-sightedness. It is the dramatic work in which the author recognizes that theater operates by a sort of magic, in which he uses his poetry to demonstrate the joyous possible in the world, the presence in the human condition of *something else*, but in which, finally, he defers to a power greater than himself.

This *something else* appears even more clearly in Coleridge's "The Nightingale." Listening at night to the song of the nightingale, Coleridge is penetrated by the unity of nature, the communion that brings together all the natural presences. He evokes a numinous moment in which nightingales, fallen silent at the moon's disappearance behind a cloud, resume singing in chorus when the moon, as it reappears, "awaken[s] earth and sky" and creates in the visible universe "one sensation." He discerns in nature "something more than nature," which urges the birds to silence in the moon's absence and fills them with joy as soon as the moon recovers its power.

He then explores this "something more," telling how he calmed the tears of his little child who had awoken, suffering, in the night. He went out of the house with him, the child saw the moon and, suddenly no longer crying, "laughs most silently." Why laughter rather than simply taking interest in a new object that draws his attention? Coleridge seems to feel, in this reaction, at first sight bizarre and excessive, in the laughter of wonderment, another sign of that intimate rapport among all the elements of nature that creates a profound and inexplicable joy. The suddenly returned song of the nightingales and the laughter of the child who cannot yet speak locate this instinctive rapport in the heart of being, far below—or beyond—reason, beyond a theory of nature everywhere living and, in a sense, supernatural. And Coleridge immediately deepens this feeling of strangeness, of what eludes us, by implicitly comparing his child's eyes and the nightingales', which "glisten" in the moonlight, and particularly by desiring that his child might grow up listening to the nocturnal song of the nightingales, "that with the night / He may associate joy." With the *night*: the converse of our habitual daytime life; with the long moment when, light having been withdrawn, the universe becomes visible.

2.

Poetry seems to me, as a poet, most capable of suggesting this joy that touches upon the supernatural. And Hebrew poetry, particularly that of the Psalms, goes even further, evoking the extraordinary and hardly conceivable joy felt by all creation. The author of Psalm 65 praises God for the work he accomplishes for the earth in soaking it with showers, clothing the prairies with flocks and the valleys with wheat, and he sees the hills "rejoice on every side." Perhaps this rejoicing is found less in the hills than the man who is contemplating them. But what then of Psalm 96, which summons all peoples to give glory and power unto the Lord, before addressing the earth itself?

> Let the heavens rejoice, and let the earth be glad!
> Let the sea roar, and the fulness thereof!
> Let the field be joyful, and all that is therein,
> then shall all the trees of the wood rejoice.
>
> (Psalm 96:11–12)

Creation is invited at the end of the poem to participate in the "new song" of the people of God with which the poem begins. As reasonable people, accustomed in Europe to a figurative and anthropomorphic poetry, we at first judge, undoubtedly, that this is a manner of speech that attributes to nature the emotions felt by the poet in order to *imagine* them—to see them in images—to share them and render them exuberant. But what if the poet really heard the trees cry out with joy—or at least perceived in them more than a vegetative life? Sensed in what we call the material world a presence, a form of joy in response to the goodness of God? In Psalm 98 also the poet wishes first to hear God praised in the sounds of the harp, of the trumpet and cornet, but this is not enough, it is too restrained. So:

> Let the sea roar, and the fulness thereof,
> the world, and they that dwell therein;
> Let the floods clap their hands;
> let the hills be joyful together.
>
> (Psalm 98:7–8)

He exhorts nature to join men in the work of praise, to second their efforts so the entire earth may come alive in gratitude, and he ends once again with joyful cries from voiceless beings, mountains as well as trees elsewhere.

This is quite curious. It would seem that the Hebrews, or their poets, discerned everywhere in the created world a great joy and that they oblige us either to read their poetry the way we read ours, in which reason or, much rather, inveterate habit does not for an instant presume that trees rejoice really, rather than only metaphorically; or else to let ourselves be drawn to an altogether different vision of reality, in which the entire creation, and not just men, is *enthusiastic* in the full meaning of the term. Carefully considered, this poetry constitutes a state of language new to us, strange, between the literal and the figurative. *Coup de foudre* has a literal meaning when lightning strikes a tree and a figurative sense when one falls suddenly in love. However, when the author of Psalm 114 affirms that at the exodus from Egypt "the mountains skipped like rams, and the little hills like lambs," he doesn't see them literally leaping, but neither does he consider the joy they are expressing as a simple metaphor. Witnessing God's saving act of Israel, those inanimate presences know an unheard-of but real joy. The vision culminates in Psalm 148, which does not mention joy but shows it, from the first verse to the last, convoking the whole creation in view of an immense choir of praise: sun, moon, sea monsters, stormy winds, mountains, hills, cedars, wild beasts, cattle, reptiles, birds, even fire, hail, snow, and mist. Everything comes alive under the gaze of the poet who, like Coleridge's little child, sees in a different way, sees better, and who hears—neither literally nor figuratively—an incommensurable praise.

The joy of the creation in the Old Testament accompanies the joy of men, which—despite catastrophes, captivities, threats of the definitive destruction of Israel, and despite cries of anguish and disarray—makes itself continually heard and can be surprisingly sweeping. It is expressed everywhere in the Psalms: "I will be glad and rejoice in thee" (Psalm 9); "In thy presence is fullness of joy" (Psalm 16); "Be glad in the Lord, and rejoice," commands Psalm 32. The author of

Psalm 43 directly addresses "God my exceeding joy." The religion of the Old Testament, in spite of the popular image of a bloody religion that a God of wrath watches over and despite the true misery of a fallen world, turns out to be a religion of joy. And this joy—a joy in God—is perhaps not the ordinary joy that we feel in the presence of joyous beings or experiences.

It recurs in the New Testament, where the reason for joy is precisely situated in the death and resurrection of the Messiah. This Christian joy, which rises from each page of the Gospel, of the Acts of the Apostles, of the epistles, of the book of Revelation, can surprise us, if we have in mind that other image of a religion of suffering, of mortification, of rejection of pleasure, of the emphasis placed insistently on sin, on the nothingness of the fallen world—an image that Christians themselves have very often propagated. Yet it suffices to leaf through the New Testament to find, for example, that Mary, having learned that she is to be the mother of Jesus, deeply moved, declares, "My spirit hath rejoiced in God my Savior" (Luke 1:47). It is natural for a young woman who is pregnant to be happy; however, her joy "in God" announces all the joy that is going to spread among the Jews and among the other peoples. And this exaltation immediately becomes a joy "beyond a common joy." The magi, having come to Palestine to contemplate him "that is born king of the Jews," as they follow his star, "rejoiced with exceeding great joy" (*charan megalèn sphodra*; Matthew 2:10) when the star stopped. Much later, Saint Peter, in his first epistle, thus addresses the Christians of the Diaspora: without seeing Christ, he writes, and yet believing, "Ye rejoice with joy unspeakable and full of glory" (*agalliasthe chara aneklalètô kai dedoxasmenè*; 1 Peter 1:8). *Very great, unspeakable and full of glory*: a joy clearly presents itself as surpassing common joy and inviting us to wonder what it consists of.

And it is also astonishing that this Christian joy is an obligation. One would expect it to be the happy consequence of faith, of love, of obedience, of a good action, but in Saint Paul's mind, to be a Christian is to be obliged to rejoice, to know an incomparable joy. After sprinkling his Epistle to the Philippians with the words *joy* and *rejoice*, he exhorts them the first time, "Rejoice in the Lord" (3:1), and then insists, "Rejoice in the Lord always and again I say, rejoice" (4:4). *Always*: it often overwhelms me to look closely at the Bible. How can one continually rejoice? And where does Paul find the confidence to impose on others this requirement, which at first glance seems impossible to fulfill? And he speaks not only to the Philippians; he also enjoins the Thessalonians with the same words, to rejoice always (1 Thessalonians 5:16). First, I believe he finds support in the experience of the Old Testament Jews, alluding to several passages and quoting the same exhortation that figures in two psalms: "Rejoice in the Lord, ye righteous" (Psalm 97:12), and "Be glad in the Lord, and rejoice, ye righteous: and shout for joy, all ye that are upright in heart" (Psalm 32:11). He understands that joy *in God* has always been a requirement, and he judges, it seems to me, that such a joy is the best path for remaining in an intimate relationship with God and with his own faith. He thus recalls another unexpected passage of the Hebrew Bible, where the people having fallen, after the solemn reading of the Law, into sadness and tears, and Ezra tells them, "Neither be ye sorry; for the joy of the Lord is your strength" (Nehemiah 8:10). Far from being a simple pleasant emotion, joy—a certain joy—protects, fortifies, is one of the royal roads toward active and continual knowledge of God. The image of the "fortress" (another translation for the Hebrew word rendered "strength" in the King James), used for joy, rather than for prudence, discipline, sobriety, is clearly food for thought. If Paul adds the idea of remaining "always" in joy, an apparently irrational vision of what is possible for us, he also finds support, undoubtedly, in his own experience, which would have taught him that, if one cannot be joyful on command, seeking joy becomes at the same time seeking God, that it recenters the person on the essential, that it opens one up to all the depth of the gospel, of the inexhaustible joy of the "good news."

3.

If one continues to explore joy in terms of Christianity, one realizes that it is also associated with the Holy Spirit. Bible readers know this, but it is useful to bring it to mind. One reads, for example, in the Acts of the Apostles that the disciples "were filled with joy, and with the Holy Ghost" (Acts 13:52). For Paul, in the Epistle to the Romans, "The kingdom of God is . . . righteousness, and peace, and joy in the Holy Ghost" (Romans 14:17); he reminds the Thessalonians that they have received the Word "in much affliction, with joy of the Holy Ghost" (1 Thessalonians 1:6). It is normal to speak constantly of the Holy Spirit in the context of conversion or sanctification, since such a presence is a part of the teaching of Jesus and the apostles. But why evoke joy so often if not to show that joy is *essential*, that it participates in the essence of the gospel and of the experience of the gospel in life. And according to the last passage quoted, joy is precisely what the Holy Spirit brings. Perhaps joy is even the *sign* of his presence.

The surprise continues when one considers, indeed, the "fruits of the Spirit." It is once again Paul who names them in the Epistle to the Galatians: "love, joy, peace, longsuffering, gentleness, goodness, faith, meekness, temperance" (Galatians 5:22–23). What does one notice? First, that all the items in the list represent what we would call, in another context, virtues, except for joy and peace, which seem to benefit in this enumeration from the same moral quality. Joy would be, not meritorious, but good: a sign indicating that one is on the right path. Then that joy occupies the second place. Even if Paul did not determine the order of these "fruits," he begins nonetheless with love, whose primacy is affirmed by the entire New Testament; how could one believe that passing directly from love to joy was not intentional?

And if joy has such importance, does it not overturn the customary priorities of Christian life? Does this importance not explain Paul's passion in telling the Thessalonians, "Rejoice evermore" (1 Thessalonians 5:16), and the Philippians, "Rejoice in the Lord always: and again I say, rejoice" (Philippians 4:4)? To associate the two perspectives—joy as an obligation and as a fruit—one penetrates also into this mysterious place where human intention meets God's action. Man cannot, on his own, rejoice in God any more than he can love God or believe in him. But if he *hears* the commandment, if he turns in that direction and accepts that possibility, he can discover in himself a joy, a love, a faith received as gifts. The whole controversy over "free will" and the "bondage of the will" is thereby clarified—as well as remaining marvelously obscure.

And how beautiful this metaphor of the fruits of the Spirit is! Which in reality form a single fruit (*karpos*). The Spirit in the life of a Christian produces spiritual fruits as a tree produces natural fruits in the life of plants. The Christian grows (ideally) like a tree. And is it really a simple metaphor? Writing to the Corinthians on the subject of the resurrection of the dead, Paul makes a comparison between a seed that, sown in the ground, is transformed into an ear of wheat and men who die with a natural body and are resurrected with a spiritual body (1 Corinthians 15:37–44). Rather than simply seek a lively and familiar way, rich in images, to speak of a subject so foreign to our experience as life after death, does he not establish a real correspondence between two parts of the divine world, where the "death and resurrection" of vegetation corresponds to that of men and where their growth corresponds to that of Christians? In a world perpetually *one* under the gaze of God and where the earth itself will be destroyed in order to reappear in the form of a "new earth," the very notion of the figurative is probably to be revised.

The evocation of this encounter of human will, responding to the exhortation to rejoice, with the divine will that alone engenders this rejoicing, prompts one to look more closely at the most frequent words in the New Testament for joy (*chara*) and for rejoice (*chairô*). For they are related to *charis*, which means both "grace" and "thankfulness." Spiritual joy appears precisely as a grace, the rapport between the two words expressing the origin of this joy in the benevolence of God. Joy, a fruit of the Spirit, is always and quite simply a grace. A joy "beyond a common joy" implies "something more than nature" and comes from elsewhere. And the word *charis* reveals, implicitly but most efficaciously, the fundamental exchange between God and men. God gives them benefit upon benefit by his *charis*, his *grace*, and they respond, according to another meaning of the word, with their own *charis*, their gratitude and their thanks. Paul (he again), who knows he has received from Jesus Christ "grace [*charin*] and apostleship" (Romans 1:5), says immediately to the beneficiaries of this calling, "I thank [*eucharistô*] my God through Jesus Christ for you all" (Romans 1:8). English—as well as other languages—has retained this double meaning as in a mirror: when we receive grace, we feel gratitude, or "say grace."

4.

The question posed at the beginning of this reflection becomes more and more pressing: how may we reconcile this joy with the world's flagrant sadness? And how can a Christian be required not only to rejoice but to rejoice continually? Both the human and the nonhuman world suffer relentlessly. The Christian, like all men, feels sickness, rejection, grief; suffers from his sins; and shares (often so little) Christ's sufferings.

The Bible clearly recognizes that this rather strange joy is compatible with suffering and implies it. We are considered "as sorrowful, yet always rejoicing" (2 Corinthians 6:10), writes Paul to the Corinthians. It is possible that he is denying being sad (that is, subject to a worldly sadness), since he's also written: considered "as deceivers, and yet true" (2 Corinthians 6:8). However, here is the end of this long passage where thought and passion are ordered by a learned rhetoric: "as sorrowful, yet always rejoicing; as poor, yet making many rich; as having nothing, and yet possessing all things" (2 Corinthians 6:10). God's servants live in paradox: really sad, poor, and impoverished and at the same time joyful, able to enrich others, and filled with spiritual wealth. They know the paradox of the cross, where the perfect Innocent became the universal Guilty. And this apostle, who never ceases to astound us, once again proclaims himself not just joyful but "always joyful." We are reduced to imagining, no doubt, this unfathomable state of being in which a continuity of joy is not lost in a profound sadness.

Other passages in Paul's letters help one partly understand this resonance between joy and sorrow. A little further in his second letter to the Corinthians, he writes, "Great is my boldness of speech toward you, great is my glorying of you: I am filled with comfort, I am exceeding joyful in all our tribulation" (2 Corinthians 7:4). It is almost simple! His joy concerning the Christians of Corinth enters into the tribulations he ceaselessly suffers and helps him bear them. He rejoices *despite* the sorrow of his uninterrupted trials. And if his joy is *always* present, it is also *exceeding*. To the Colossians he speaks thus: I "now rejoice [*chairô*] in my sufferings for you" (Colossians 1:24). To rejoice in one's sufferings is here at opposite poles from the pathological disturbance whose origin is in the power of sin. Paul is happy to be able to suffer for Christians for whom he feels responsible, knowing that his suffering participates in the love he feels for them. But these perspectives on joy hardly exhaust its meaning and do not permit us fully to grasp a joy that does not exist *despite* suffering and that does not find its explanation in its unfolding within brotherly love—which exists rather in itself and as paradox.

One approaches it more closely in reading a well-known passage of Paul's letter to the Philippians, a passage that does not mention joy but that gains increased power from its appearing in the text that insists most often and with the most fervor on joy, on the obligation to experience it and on its continual presence. I desire one thing, he writes to them, "that I may know him [Christ], and the power of his resurrection, and the fellowship of his sufferings, being made conformable unto his death; if by any means I might attain unto the resurrection of the dead" (Philippians 3:10–11). The sufferings are first those of Christ, with which the apostle wishes to be in communion, what he suffers not coming from himself, not having its seat in his own sensibility, but coming from his relationship with the Other—*being* the suffering of the Other. And what are these sufferings, insofar as we are capable of conceiving them? Most likely all the results of sin, of the fallen condition of men and the world. Jesus shows during his life his sadness at grief, weeping over Lazarus's death; his sadness at not being able to gather the inhabitants of Jerusalem under his wings, as a hen her chicks; his sorrow at seeing his disciples' lack of faith; his indignant sorrow before the hypocrisy of the scribes and Pharisees. Beyond all particular sadness, and before bearing the burden of all the world's sins, he had to suffer for the perversion of the whole creation, for the great rejection—whether indifferent or hateful—of eternal love, and at the same time for men's suffering in their bitterness and confusion. Paul wished to know this, by sinking, not into himself, but into a vertiginous and fearful relationship with Christ.

A certain suffering proves necessary, just as is necessary a certain joy. And the desire for suffering is accompanied in Paul by a no less imperious desire to know the power of the resurrection, with the joy it brings. He even uses a significant chiasmus: resurrection—sufferings—death—resurrection. The power of the resurrection gives him the power to plunge into sufferings and death, and this plunge prepares him for the resurrection to life. Joy and suffering mutually strengthen one another. The more one experiences, if I may say so, the right kind of suffering, that which comes from Christ and is marked by the divine, the more one experiences the right kind of joy. The opposite must be equally true. And this suffering and this joy are *other*. If the suffering is that of Christ, one of the resurrection narratives also places joy in a context that suggests its numinous nature. Mary Magdalene and Mary, mother of James, having come to see Jesus's tomb, learn through an angel that he is risen. Troubled by the vision of the angel, the earthquake that accompanied his descent from heaven, and the inconceivable news of the resurrection from the dead, they depart "with fear [*phobon*] and great joy [*charas*]" (Matthew 28:8). Far from being a simple fright, this fear is a profound religious awe, the fear, the *phobos* that Aristotle identifies, along with pity, as the principal emotion aroused by tragedy. The association of fear and joy in the two Marys' reaction—in their being—signals that the joy participates in this gravity, in this sudden amplification of vision produced by the intervention of another world, of a new perspective on life.

5.

And could not the joy that I am struggling to understand, the joy that, far from being a pure emotion, touches upon what transcends the human, be finally the joy of Christ? When one listens to them attentively, the passages of John's Gospel that speak of it open one's spirit to the infinite. Having invited the disciples to remain in his love by keeping his commandments, Jesus continues: "These things have I spoken unto you, that my joy might remain in you, and that your joy might be full" (John 15:11). He offers them, not simply a very great joy, but his own joy, unimaginable, divine. The Christian is inhabited, in a more or less strong way, by the very joy of Jesus, which, far from being an intrusion, becomes also the Christian's joy: "my joy . . . your joy." Jesus remembers these words in his long prayer to the Father: "And now come I to thee; and these things I speak in the world, that they might have my joy fulfilled in themselves" (John 17:13). The Gospel writer undoubtedly includes the two moments so as to emphasize the importance and the extraordinary character of this gift. (It is again John who records Jesus's comparable words concerning peace: "Peace I leave with you, my peace I give unto you"; John 14:27.) True joy is indeed supernatural. It is no more to be confused with natural joy than true love with that which we can find within us, or true faith with that which is in our power to exercise. At the same time, even as the love that only God can give us is nevertheless *our* love, and as the faith—which we are not capable of and we receive as a gift—is *our* faith, this joy is thus *our* joy. The mystery of this relationship is not explainable by the would-be doctrine of cooperation between grace and nature. It is accomplished in an affirmation by Paul: "I live; yet not I, but Christ liveth in me" (Galatians 2:20). It is Christ who lives, but *in me*.

Here finally is the *excessive* joy, the joy that exists "beyond a common joy"—the joy of the Son of God. If the Christian can and must know the fellowship of his sufferings, he is called to participate just as much in his joy. And to attune himself, it seems, to the joy of heaven. As to reacting to earthly events, Jesus evokes the "joy [which] shall be in heaven" at the moment when a sinner repents (Luke 15:7). (We probably do not think enough about this expansion of our horizon represented by the continuous comings and goings between heaven and earth.) As to heaven at the end time, the author of Revelation in his vision hears an innumerable crowd crying out, when the Lord takes possession of his reign: "Let us be glad and rejoice, and give honor to him: for the marriage of the Lamb is come" (Revelation 19:7). The idea is familiar, but not the fact that joy beats in the heart of the most elevated things. Joy is fundamental. Perhaps it would not be false to say that God *is* joy. Here is the ultimate justification for Paul's exhortation: "Rejoice in the Lord *always*." And here is the basis for Pascal's experience, which he wrote down in the "memorial" found after his death, sewn into his jacket, containing the following words: "Certitude, certitude, feeling, joy, peace. . . . Joy, joy, joy, tears of joy. . . . Eternally in joy for a day's exercise on the earth." And here is the true gift of the incarnation, grasped with force and emotion in a single line of *Piers Plowman*. God "risked himself" in the incarnation, writes the author, "To wite what al wo is that wote of al Ioye," to know all suffering, he who knew all joy.

As I have said, this orientation toward joy hardly corresponds to a certain way of presenting Christianity. Joy does not figure among the entries in the otherwise extremely useful *Dictionnaire critique de théologie* by Jean-Yves Lacoste. Neither does it appear in the index, except under the form of *messianic joy*, which refers us to *Beatitude*. One would need to hear again the apostle's injunction to live joyfully, trying to understand it and put it into relationship with the body of commandments and invitations governing the Christian's life. It certainly is not a matter of seeking joy directly by considering it an end in itself, just as it is useless to seek happiness rather than that which makes one happy. However, if I am not mistaken, joy is not a simple product of what makes us joyful, the way a carpenter's happiness is the product of his love of carpentry. For Spinoza, it is indeed the fundamental orientation of life, which is expressed by acting well and by joy, but in the same way that the fact of acting in harmony with the truth of "God" and of the world gives joy, joy gives in return the possibility of acting well. According to a well-known phrase, it is "man's passing from a lesser perfection to a greater," since, contrary to sadness, it increases the power of spirit and body. Acting well and joy are both obligations created by the nature of things. For Saint Paul (who would immediately see the limitations at the base of the philosophers' and the world's vision of God), it is indeed obedience to Christ that gives joy, but the exhortation does not come in the form of "serve the Lord and you will rejoice." Rejoicing in the Lord forms an indivisible whole; the Christian is supposed to seek Christ *in a certain way*, by appreciating what, in Christ and in his relationship with us, is joyous. Must we not think that even the aspiration to become conformed to his death, to share the fellowship of his sufferings, does not exclude joy but assumes it?

But just how can this entire reflection on joy, conducted from a Christian perspective, interest those who are indifferent to Christianity? In this way, it seems to me: we know that misery is everywhere, that *the world as it goes*[6] is not going well, but here is the strong vision of a possible joy, of a joy that even transcends the certain but provisional joys that life ordinarily offers us. A mysterious joy, that of the earth, of the trees, and of the mountains, of the inhabitants of heaven, of the Holy Spirit, of Christ. The real joy of whoever really suffers. It does not deny our misfortunes; it encompasses them. It is, for our accustomed gaze, the other side of things, like the night sky in relation to the veil of blue or clouds that protects us during the day. The *something else* that one feels in reality, associated with the Man both same and other who makes all the difference. A joy partly here, above all elsewhere, in the beyond of death.

---

6 Voltaire wrote a philosophical tale titled "Le Monde comme il va" (The World as It Goes).

4

Of (Not So) Numerous Words

1.

This *something else* that joy reveals and from which it emanates is the kingdom of heaven, which crosses our reality, occasionally making itself felt. It is infinitely close; we enter it through the Lord's Prayer.

But do Christians know that in reciting it, they are reciting a poem? And having learned that—by reflecting on the rhythm that guides them in the prayer, or by reading it arranged in verse in the recent translations of the Bible—do they remain perplexed or even disappointed? Why would the most fundamental of prayers be a poem? And doesn't this poem, deprived of images and of so many beauties normally associated with poetry, seem, from that angle, a bit prosaic?

To respond to that possible concern, it is not enough to advance spiritual arguments, no matter how decisive in their way. It is certain

that the poem is severe because it concentrates the attention of the
"new man," in whom still dwells the sinful "old man," on the essen-
tial. Its brevity is explained by this injunction from Qoheleth: "Be
not rash with thy mouth, and let not thine heart be hasty to utter
anything before God; for God is in heaven, and thou upon earth;
therefore, let thy words be few" (Ecclesiastes 5:2). In order to *appre-
ciate* the Lord's Prayer as a poem and grasp the indissoluble link
between the poetic and the spiritual, we must rather relearn how
to read it.

Let us begin with the poem's structure, by patterning the
English translation on the Greek of Matthew 6:9–13:

Father of-us which art in heaven,
Be-hallowed the name of-Thee.
Come the kingdom of-Thee,
Be-done the will of-Thee
As in heaven, so on earth.
The bread of-us the daily (?) give us today.
And forgive us the debts of-us,
As we forgive the debtors of-us.
And lead us not into temptation,
But deliver us from evil [or the Evil One].

Twisting English this way in order to allow a perfectly natu-
ral verbal arrangement in Greek (which writes, for example, not
Thy name but *the name of-Thee*) to come through certainly has the
immediate effect of rendering the poem as unpoetic as possible!
However, one thereby perceives without difficulty the parallelism
of Hebrew poetry. The first three requests follow the form of syn-
onymic parallelism with variations, each desiring the same thing
from a slightly different point of view. They recall numerous exam-
ples in the Old Testament of this simple and vigorous procedure:

"When Israel went out of Egypt, / The house of Jacob from a people of strange language" or "the mountains skipped like rams, / and the little hills like lambs" (Psalm 114:1, 4), and particularly this one:

> I will praise thee, O Lord, among the people;
> I will sing unto thee among the nations.
> For thy mercy is great unto the heavens,
> And thy truth unto the clouds.
> Be thou exalted, O God, above the heavens;
> Let thy glory be above all the earth!
>
> (Psalm 57:9–11; 108:3–5)

One also sees, in this intentionally awkward translation, a form that is repeated with an exactitude pleasing to the ear as well as the mind: "Be-hallowed | the name | of-Thee," "Come the kingdom | of-Thee," "Be-done | the will | of Thee." And one discerns, in the Greek "verses" conforming to the ways of Hebrew poetry, a rhythm borne by two strong accents put at the same places:

> *hagiasthètô to onoma sou*
> *elthetô hè basileia sou*
> *genèthètô to thelèma sou*

The words begin to sing.

Of the four other requests, the first two correspond by their wording to synthetic or constructive parallelism, "give us our bread / forgive us our debts," and the last two to antithetical parallelism, "lead us not into temptation / but deliver us from evil." The second creates, with the stich that completes it, a kind of semantic rhyme: "the debts of-us / the debtors of-us" (*ta opheilèmata hèmôn / tois opheiletais hèmôn*). (In the shorter version of the prayer given in Luke 11:2–4, one finds *sins* in place of *debts*.)

The language of the Lord's Prayer reveals itself to be finely crafted, according to a prosody that is above all syntactic and semantic. Matthew's Greek, translating Jesus's Aramaic, seeks the form but also the rhythm and sonorities of this renewed language of poetry. Perhaps even a warning Jesus gives just before the prayer helps us understand the repetitive structure: "When ye pray, use not vain repetitions, as the heathen do" (Matthew 6:7). Explaining from another angle the extreme conciseness of the poem, he also clarifies the completely different kind of repetition in the first three requests, which invite us to concentrate on God's sovereign glory and to enter ever more deeply into it—a repetition, not vain and tiresome, but creative of a more and more attentive consciousness. The words of the prayer are finally *very* numerous, in the other sense of the word: harmonious, rhythmic.

The passages preceding and following the prayer demand indeed to be taken into consideration; they can enrich the prayer when we say it. One knows the importance of Jesus's words in verse 8, "Your Father knoweth what things ye have need of, before ye ask him," which illuminate (with a light partly opaque for our fallen intelligence) the very nature of prayer. One knows that he comments, immediately after the prayer, on the remission of debts: "If ye forgive men their trespasses, your heavenly Father will also forgive you; but if ye forgive not men their trespasses, neither will your Father forgive your trespasses" (Matthew 6:14–15). The commandment in verse 20—"Lay up for yourselves treasures in heaven, . . . for where your treasure is, there will your heart be also"—explains *our* interest, so to speak, in the first three requests. The one in verse 33— "Seek ye first the kingdom of God and his righteousness, and all these things shall be added unto you"—clarifies this same interest from another point of view. If Jesus chooses—in order to support an astounding promise, "Ask and it shall be given you"—the example of the man who would not give his son a stone if he asked for bread (Matthew 7:9–10), it is while reminding us of the first request that concerns us directly. The Lord's Prayer is a short poem that draws from what precedes it and radiates out onto what follows, a little like a determining line in theater.

2.

But for the time being, we are only on the threshold of the poem; another preceding passage gives access to it: "When thou prayest, thou shalt not be as the hypocrites. . . . But thou, when thou prayest, enter into thy closet, and when thou hast shut thy door, pray to thy Father which is in secret; and thy Father which seeth in secret shall reward thee openly" (Matthew 6:5–6). He has already commanded not to give alms in such a way as to be seen and approved by men, and he will say the same about fasting. Each of the three passages ends in exactly the same series of words: act "in secret; and thy Father which seeth in secret shall reward thee openly"; even in the prose surrounding the prayer that he is teaching us, Jesus makes his words resound in a form. And the verse on the secret nature of prayer, quoting the Old Testament, makes the situations to which he is referring present in our minds, it seems to me. In 2 Kings, Elisha, having arrived in a dead child's room, "went in therefore, and shut the door upon them twain, and prayed unto the Lord" (2 Kings 4:33). A passage of Isaiah addresses the faithful thus: "Come, my people, enter thou into thy chambers, / and shut thy doors about thee: / hide thyself as it were for a little moment, / until the indignation be overpast. / For, behold, the Lord cometh out of his place / to punish the inhabitants of the earth for their iniquity" (Isaiah 26:20–21). Why recall these moments, apparently very foreign to the situation of someone praying the Lord's Prayer? Matthew recalls them clearly, using in both cases the Greek of the Septuagint. Could it be that we retire, not exactly like Elisha to

raise the dead, but in order for our relationship with God to raise us
from spiritual death and prepare us for the resurrection of the end
time? And for our isolation in prayer to protect us from the wrath
of God against sin, encouraging us to beg him to forgive us and
strengthen us against temptation? (In the verse preceding this pas-
sage of Isaiah, one reads, "Thy dead men shall live, together with
my dead body shall they arise.")

These words on secrecy enrich the prayer from the very first
verse and change our sense of the real in a vertiginous fashion. "Our
Father" places us suddenly in an incommensurable world of eter-
nity and vastness. "Father" opens up above us a kind of infinite
verticality, "our" causes to pass through our individuality an almost
limitless horizontality of other beings in prayer. When we then say,
alone in our room with the door shut, "who art in heaven," as well
as recalling the affirmation that the Father is with us in this secret
place, is our world not turned upside down? Are we not gaining
passage into a great mystery? If Ecclesiastes warns us of the distance
that separates us from God and separates heaven from earth—"God
is in heaven, and thou upon earth"—the Lord's Prayer shows us
that, in another light, God is here and heaven surrounds us. "Pray
to thy Father which is . . . in thy closet," says Jesus, slipping into the
familiar form of second-person address, from *your* to *thy* in order
to speak of this moment of intimacy. Thanks to the beginning of
the poem, whose already extraordinary resonance is increased by the
introductory and accompanying prose that is so well integrated,
we pray to a God who is there, with us in the secret of a private
place, and we proclaim that he is in the heavens. In a sense, we
already know this: "Wherever God is," says Saint Theresa of Avila,
"there is heaven," and God is everywhere.[1] But are we conscious of
this? Pronouncing these words, in this context and day after day,

---

1   See Theresa of Avila, *The Way of Perfection*, ch. 28.

makes us sensitive to the presence of heaven in the here and now, like an invisible immensity that presses in on us from all sides. Each moment stretches out to infinity.

As at the beginning of any great poem, a door is opened onto another world, or a world that is other. The first request prolongs and augments the wonderment; even when having become familiar, it does not cease to surprise us: "Hallowed be thy name." Even though we know that, for the Jews whom Jesus was addressing, to wish that the "name" of God be "hallowed" was in no way unusual, still the two words are situated beyond our reach, and the Jews must have realized it each time they seriously reflected on them. Of the holiness of God, the "inaccessible dwelling of his mystery," according to the beautiful expression of the *Catechism of the Catholic Church* (§2809), we only know that it must be radiant in all his creatures. And we hear in our spirit, or in the Spirit, an enormous sound, the incessant choir of heavenly and earthly inhabitants already glorifying God, with whom we join. To say "Hallowed be thy name" is to make one's room resound with the voices of angels and saints in paradise and of the sea, the countryside, the trees (Psalm 96). The "feeling of presence" created, according to Henri Bremond, by all true poetry attains here its apogee, in this universe of speakers, of singers that suddenly surrounds us.

A few words are enough for everyday reality to be entirely transformed, for the blindness and deafness that prevent us from seeing and hearing to be in the blink of an eye, albeit very partially, healed. The first virtue of poetry would be to change our manner of grasping the real, as a foretaste of its veritable change at the end of time, and the poem we are reciting as we repeat the Lord's Prayer is not only in the highest degree Christian, but *Christian* in the fullest sense, since we pronounce the verses composed and spoken by Christ, who knows the astonishing reality and offers it to us.

I have said that the poem is vertiginous, and, after other verses enlarge our shrunken world—"thy kingdom come, thy will be done"—we descend abruptly into the known reality: "on earth as it is in heaven." The vertiginous quality of this is better indicated in Greek, which places the comparison first: "as in heaven, also on earth," and I do not see why the contrary rule in English would prevent us from following what in this case is a far more expressive order. Since these words may well apply to the three requests we have just formulated, our wish would cause to arrive on the earth, along with the will of God, the hallowing of his name and the coming of his kingdom. The entire first part of the prayer, divine, celestial, descends among us. The change of perspective is immediately underlined by the first of the four petitions concerning us: "Give us this day our daily bread"—by the appearance of this common and familiar bread. If poetry offers us a glimpse of another world, of a reality more real at the heart of reality, it does not distance us from the known world: it makes the ordinary extraordinary, in all its details, it shows us that it is here that is being prepared the transformation of the created world into a new heaven and a new earth. We suddenly find ourselves in the material world, as well as in the passing of time, in the present of "today." And how attractive and humbly tangible this bread appears after the voyage into the sublime! And how its presence rejoices us! The word *bread* is even poetic in a sense of the word that modern reflections on poetry have brought into the light: it is suggestive. While remaining simply bread, it makes us think of the manna of the Old Testament, which is also daily, of the word of God, of Jesus as the bread of life.

Finally, this second part of the prayer—after having brought us back to the reality that we know well, to our hungers of all kinds, to our sins, to the forgiveness that we beg for and that we are slow to give, to temptation—plunges us anew into what transcends us, when we ask to be delivered from evil, or from the Evil One.

In Greek, the poem begins with the word "God" and ends with the word "evil." It moves forward between the two extreme poles of our unknowing. Despite its brevity, it contains everything, and its form is perfect.

3.

The Lord's Prayer resembles the closed room where Jesus commands us to say it: it too is a little place trembling with the gathering of the worlds and their creator. And if this poem recreates the real in the perception that we have of it, it also recreates our self, according to another virtue of poetry. Transforming our vision of the world and radically changing us ourselves for the greater glory of God seems indeed to be its objective. The self is everywhere in question. In the first three requests, before praying for ourselves, we necessarily reflect on the sincerity of our words. The first reaction to the strange glory of the first verse, "Our Father, which art in heaven"—a reaction of astonishment, of gratitude—is the wish for the name of the Father to be hallowed. In saying this, we realize that we desire it, certainly, but quite weakly, that it is hardly the focus of our life, that among the thousand things we do each day, hallowing God's name is probably, alas, the last of our worries. The requests become increasingly constraining. "Thy kingdom come," yes, at the end of time, and even now in the lives of Christians in general, and somewhat in mine. "Thy will be done," certainly, as an admirable idea, but may my own not be too hindered. These requests—if we go more deeply into them day after day as we go more deeply, through a meticulously attentive reading, into each verse of a great poem—educate us. They show that we must not wish, for example, for God's will to be done only because that would be right, but, on an entirely different level, because God is our Father and we love him. According to Thomas Aquinas, the Lord's Prayer "teaches us to ask, but it also forms our affectivity." To say this prayer regularly, both at home and in worship, is to become little by little a person who is *capable* of saying it.

And if the three requests that concern primarily the holy and sovereign Father lead us to reflect on ourselves, the last four, which concern us directly, bring us nevertheless out of ourselves by opening us to God and to others. We begin by recalling our need, asking for bread, in a "today" that seems brusquely to distance us from the eternity of God. The imitation in Greek of the repeated Hebrew *and*—"Give us . . . our bread . . . *and* forgive us our debts . . . *and* lead us not into temptation"—stresses the multiplicity of our needs; the present bread, the past debts, and the temptation that threatens us in the future extend our need over the three dimensions of time that we understand. But to ask for our bread directs our attention less to ourselves than to our confidence in God, as the "daily" bread invites us to rest in God for tomorrow; to beg forgiveness directs us to the mercy of God and to others whose offenses we are to pardon; to pray for deliverance orients us to the sanctifying and saving God. The whole poem draws us outward so as to transform us inwardly. The more we look at others, the more our self blossoms; the more we become conscious of who we are, the better we see what is not us. Introspection and extraspection work together.

And who is speaking when we pray the Lord's Prayer? Is it not curious that "I" is entirely absent from the prayer Jesus gives us? I withdraw to my room, and I say "we." Even the word *our* changes continually in meaning, as if to make us reflect on our relationship with ourselves and others. Our Father is not one of our possessions, our bread comes as a gift, only our debts and our sins belong to us. To repeat this plural, from the beginning right to the end of the prayer, teaches us that each person's *I is* essentially only in relationship with a *we* that transcends and embraces it. I am, but only because the *we* of Christians supports me, and on condition of recognizing this. Hence the force of this verse in particular: "Forgive us our debts / as we forgive our debtors." The relationship to others becomes both explicit and particularly urgent.

And there is more: Who is saying "Father?" The person who is praying, obviously, but the question is more complex. If Saint Paul writes in his letter to the Romans, "Ye have received the Spirit of adoption, whereby we cry, Abba! Father!" (Romans 8:15), he also writes in his letter to the Galatians, "God hath sent forth his Son into your hearts, crying Abba! Father!" (Galatians 4:6). We speak, but it is rather the Spirit who speaks in us. As, again according to Paul, it is no longer quite we who live but Christ who lives within us (Galatians 2:20). Toward the end of the *Four Quartets*, the great Christian poem by T. S. Eliot published in 1944, a narrator tells how at the beginning of an encounter with a person from another world, "I . . . cried / And heard another's voice cry." Here is the fundamental experience of the poet: discovering that it is not exactly he who composes his poem, that another speaks within him, and that he becomes other in the act of writing. This lesson from poetry helps us better understand the singular condition of the Christian. The fact that one becomes, in some way, the voice of the Holy Spirit and that one is transformed into someone else while speaking clarifies in return the poet's experience, as well as the reader's. In the everlastingly strange poem that is the Lord's Prayer, pronounced at the same time by myself and an Other, we are provisionally, and perhaps actually, in the long run, other and better.

4.

Poetry, which always requires from the poet and the reader a more sustained attention, a new mode of being, finds in the Lord's Prayer its astonishing apogee. It has for its third virtue that of transforming language. In saying this prayer, we enter into a renewed

language. We come to it, moreover, from prose, from Jesus's words
by which he prepares us, and we have the impression, when the first
verse (as one says in music) strikes up—"Our Father, which art in
heaven"—of penetrating suddenly into the world of poetry. (In cer-
tain of Shakespeare's plays also, the spectator crosses the threshold
of a new world when the author makes him pass from prose to the
differently cadenced language of verse.) The rhythms, the syntactic
forms that recur, and sounds that reply, in Greek, to one another,
constitute the veiled vision and more precisely the faint hearing of
a language recreated and saved from the fall. In this rare world,
we even encounter a word, *epiousios*, that confounds the transla-
tors. Matthew or Luke seems to have invented it exclusively for this
prayer; people don't know quite how to translate it; they opt tradi-
tionally for *daily*, while noting that *necessary to subsistence, tomor-
row's* and *the next day's* are also possible. It is a bit disconcerting,
particularly when it occurs at the moment when, with the request
for bread, we abruptly descend from the heights of the name, of the
kingdom, and of the will of God into the earthliest reality. Why
does the text leave us an enigma, if not perhaps that we might pen-
etrate the extraordinary nature of this prayer that has become so
habitual and that we might see in this assuredly *other* word the sign
of a truly renewed language?

If all great poetry results, whatever the poet's intention, in
transforming the real in our eyes, in transforming us and the lan-
guage we speak, the three transformations mutually reinforcing
one another, then the Lord's Prayer—in a religion whose principle,
during the time elapsing between the fall and the end of the world,
is to transform everything—is found at the heart of poetry. And
Jesus is its poet. Upon reading especially Luke's account, where one
of the disciples asks Jesus to teach them to pray (Luke 11:1), we
could meditate on the remarkable fact that he gives them a poem
in reply. He often speaks in verse, following the norms of Hebrew

poetry; he thus prolongs and completes the wisdom teachings of the Old Testament. His "poem" on the beatitudes is a word that dances. It would not be false to conclude that, while pursuing an infinitely more elevated calling, he contributed to his people's culture. His composition of the Lord's Prayer is extremely accurate; it demands our attentive hearing and, when we study it, a rigorous analysis that takes into account the perfect unity of the spiritual and the poetic.

The great prayer should always surprise us. For example, a lone object is mentioned, our conscience being filled above all with the things of the spirit. This bread—alone among the hallowing of a name, the kingdom, the will, the forgiveness of debts, temptation, evil—seems that much more present, like a reminder, both sober and warm, of the concrete world where salvation is accomplished. The poem extends between the two words "Father" and (according to one possible translation) "Evil One," in a pedagogical hesitation between the complete confidence we have in God and the mistrust we appropriately feel for ourselves. The doxology that ends the prayer—"For thine is the kingdom and the power and the glory forever"—though it seems to be a late gloss, has as its consequence, and had perhaps originally as its function, to connect the Lord's Prayer to those psalms that descend into human misery before a happy conclusion reassures and rejoices us.

One is struck especially, on stepping back from the poem, by the absence of any reference to love. Shouldn't the prayer taught by Jesus have at its heart the love of God and of one's neighbor? But love permeates the whole of this basically allusive and ingenious poem. The first three requests motivate us to desire the hallowing of God's name, the arrival of his kingdom, and the accomplishment of his will, not only (as I have said) because this is right, but because we love him and wish, for his sake, these things to happen. The love of God is implied in the tender words "Our Father," and the love of our neighbor is concentrated in a hardly fathomable series of words: "as we forgive our debtors." But we would not have thus imagined the most essential of prayers! With petitions such as "help us love you," "make us compassionate," "touch us in our inward parts," we could have imagined a very different poem—passionate and immediately inspiring. In the secret place of prayer, Jesus brings us to *impersonalize* ourselves so that our affections and our deep will might arise from a heightened attention. The prayer is curiously practical; while offering itself to the entire world, it is founded on the wise realism of the Hebrews.

The prayer, without speaking of love, is nonetheless a love poem, where everything is given in the first two words. Just as the Song of Songs is, according to the superlative form in Hebrew, the most beautiful of songs, the brief and yet boundless poem that is the Lord's Prayer, the prayer of prayers, is the most beautiful of poems.

5

Incarnation and Culture

1.

The Lord's Prayer reveals, surrounding the praying person, an unmeasurable world, where the natural and the supernatural, the temporal and the spiritual, are joined. We recite it behind a "shut door," yet it tears us away from ourselves, turning us toward God and others. What, then, is the relationship between this divine milieu and the culture that supports Christians and solicits them? In view of the untimely nature of Christianity, one must expect both close and distant relations.

Does not culture from a Christian perspective—through literature, painting, music—give testimony first to the world's irresistible attractiveness and to life's happiness? Does it not react as well to the world's disgrace and to life's affliction, to a fallen reality in which history teaches us that we are continuing to fall? And does it not give itself above all, by taking the measure of the catastrophe, to transcending it, to accomplishing or imagining a profound change? Since the beginning is lost and the present torn between wonderment and horror, it aims at a new beginning. Whence the successive schools in the arts, in philosophy, anthropology, historiography, sociology, linguistics that attest at once to our inexhaustible creativity; to the continual, restless, and innovative metamorphosis of society, as of the experience of the generations; and to the fact that the goal is never attained. Culture is everything by which we try to praise our world, to understand its decadence, and to remedy it. It is the set of means by which we explore our feeling that life should not be such as we know it and our intuition of what it could be. At the heart of Greek civilization stands Greek tragedy, which probes the grandeur and misery of man, to use the ever-living vocabulary of Pascal, and which seeks obstinately something beyond misfortune. At the heart of the Jewish Bible one sings of God, the creation, and man; one anguishes over sin, death, and an unfaithful people; and one awaits the Messiah, a "new heaven," and a "new earth."

At first glance, all of culture, then, should be open to the gospel, which explains the happiness and the misery of our condition, which responds to our desire for *something else*, and which concentrates our attention fully on the life, death, and resurrection of Jesus. Whether or not we recognize it, whether or not we wish it, Christ is at the heart of all our cultures. However, we know very well that contemporary culture is opposed to Christianity, as much by its hostility as by its indifference. As opposed to satire, which serves to unmask the practices of a sick world, it is characterized by derision, which scouts the world and its problems. By incredulity also, as recommended by a venerable postmodernism, regarding all metanarratives, all global explanations of history and of humanity's destination. And often by the rejection of the very idea of an objective truth independent of our opinions, in favor of an equivalence of all fixed positions and all value systems. Despite our society's disarray, despite our contemporaries' feeling of having lost the meaning of life and the hope of a better future, the moment does not seem propitious for evangelization.

But the moment is never propitious! The gospel was first proclaimed in a Jewish society that resisted it and in a Greek world founded on ideas and values for which such a message appeared "foolishness" (1 Corinthians 1:23). The very first one to bring the "good news," Christ himself, was crucified. The world is still the world; Christianity still constitutes, without arrogance or scorn, a counterculture.

Whence the interest in Paul's behavior toward the Jews and Greeks, as it is recounted by Luke in the Acts of the Apostles, chapter 17. In the synagogue in Thessalonica, one reads that for three successive Sabbaths, he "reasoned with them [the Jews] out of the scriptures. Opening and alleging, that Christ must needs have suffered, and risen again from the dead; and that this Jesus, whom I preach unto you, is Christ" (Acts 17:2–3). He offers them a new perspective on their culture, without any compromise with their own interpretation and ending with the essential, the death and marvelously implausible resurrection of Jesus. In Athens, he proceeds in almost the same way in his famous speech before the Areopagus. To the Greeks also he proposes an altogether different perspective on the culture to which they are accustomed. Seeing that their superstition extends so far as to erect an altar "to the unknown god" (Acts 17:23), he declares to them this God whom they do not know, "Lord of heaven and earth" (Acts 17:24) and master of history (Acts 17:26). Recalling a passage found in two Greek poets, "We are also of his offspring" (Acts 17:28), he affirms that this relationship that we have with God renders idols absurd and, since "in him we live and move and have our being," that it is incumbent upon us not to reflect about him but to seek him. He closes once again by announcing something that contradicts the entire orientation of their thought: the necessity of repenting, the judgment to come, and the

resurrection. Some of his listeners, scoffing at the resurrection from
the dead, show the frivolity of seeking novelty motivated by sim-
ple curiosity, Luke having informed us that the Athenians and the
foreigners residing among them were always wishing to tell or hear
"some new thing" (Acts 17:21). When they are presented with the
truly new thing, the newly true thing that would have changed
everything for them, they do not recognize it.

Paul makes no concession to the Athenians. He observes and
quotes their culture but does not stroke their vanity. He shows them
that if they are "too superstitious" (or better, "very religious"—the
expression is ironic; Acts 17:22), they do not know God and that
their great culture does not prevent them from being in "igno-
rance" (Acts 17:30). (It is extraordinary: in the eyes of the gospel,
the ancient culture that we regard as the most learned is in reality
ignorant.) He does not present the gospel as credible, any more
than God was not concerned with the credibility of his prom-
ise when he declared to Abraham, too old to have children, that
he would be the father of an innumerable progeny. He teaches
strange things—repentance, the judgment of the universe, the res-
urrection of the dead—without seeking more or less equivalent
notions in Greek thought that would make them intelligible and
appropriable. Here is an important lesson for reflecting on evan-
gelization and culture. It indicates that it would be counterpro-
ductive and even unfaithful to the message to try to prepare one's
listeners this way. The gospel *is not* credible, except for those to
whom faith is given.

Yes, but what if his sermon was a failure? That is said some-
times, from two opposite points of view. It is contended that the
first encounter of Christianity and Hellenism, of Paul and Athens,
was not a success. To judge this way is to assume that Paul should
have had the ambition to reveal to the Athenians that their culture
was compatible with that of Christians in order that the gospel might

slip almost imperceptibly into the Greek mind. But such was not his intention, either in Athens or elsewhere. It is true that he does not found a church in Athens, but in the cities where his message was received, there is never any question of a happy marriage between the faith and the local culture. The other objection is more thought-provoking: Paul fails, it is said, because he uses the accouterments of Greek wisdom instead of concentrating exclusively on the gospel. He must have later realized his error, since he wrote to other Greeks at the church in Corinth that he had founded, "I came to you . . . not with excellency of speech or of wisdom, declaring unto you the testimony of God. For I determined not to know anything among you, save Jesus Christ, and him crucified" (1 Corinthians 2:1–2). Perhaps the objection is valid. Paul certainly had no need to lead the Athenians toward the truth of the gospel by starting with what they already were thinking. He was using his knowledge of the Athenians' customs to begin his evangelization by having a daily discussion on the agora with the passersby (in the same manner that later, in Ephesus, he taught for two years in the school of Tyrannus; Acts 19:9), and that was sufficient for him to initiate contact. However, because of the brief outline of his speech furnished by the text, we do not know everything he said once he had arrived at the essentials—repentance, judgment, and resurrection—and we do not know what took place in Athens after his departure. And the narrative ends this way: "Howbeit certain men clave unto him, and believed: among the which was Dionysius the Areopagite, and a woman named Damaris, and others with them" (Acts 17:34). So some conversions did take place and the author furnishes—for once only during the book of Acts—the names of two converts, knowing undoubtedly that they had had, afterward, an important role. The conversion of a member of the Areopagus, the high council of Athens, seems particularly significant to him and indicates perhaps that Luke—and God—did not consider Paul's efforts to have been in vain! The mention of these names reminds us also that it is not primarily cultures we must evangelize but people.

2.

Paul preaches in a culture where the gospel is unknown and is immediately contested; grace touches several of his hearers. His practice serves as a model for the evangelization of today's Western countries, where some adhere, as in Greece, to different religions and others are persuaded that they have gone beyond Christianity and anything "religious." He will affirm to the Corinthians that he had addressed them "in weakness, and in fear, and in much trembling" given the gravity and eternity of what was at stake in his message, his preaching being thus a "demonstration of the Spirit" and of "the power of God" (1 Corinthians 2:3–5).

And his message—ours—is not about a faraway God but the incarnate Christ, who knew human life among us, for a season and forever. Nothing human is foreign to him; he knows the totality of our experience, and Son of Man and Son of God, he knows it more profoundly than we do.

He knows the simple pleasure of being alive. In order to make the famous comparison between Solomon and the lilies of the field, adorned even more gloriously (Matthew 6:28–29), he had to observe those flowers and delight in them. In the midst of his anger against Jerusalem, who kills the prophets and stones those who are sent to her, he thinks this way of his desire to save the city: "How often would I have gathered thy children together, even as a hen gathereth her chickens under her wings" (Matthew 23:37; Luke 13:34). He tastes this quite human pleasure of seeing himself figuratively, in an image touching in its candor. Even after the crucifixion, the descent into hell, and the resurrection, some of his disciples find him on the shore of a lake, with "a fire of coals there, and fish laid thereon, and bread" (John 21:9), and he invites them to breakfast.

If he knows the happiness that remains to us from Eden, he knows as well all the effects of the fall. He knows bitter disappointment when, "sorrowful, even unto death," he asks three of his disciples to wait up with him but finds them asleep (Matthew 26:36–40). He knows grief at Lazarus's death; otherwise, why would he shed tears (John 11:35), knowing that he is going to raise him? Seeing the grief-stricken sorrow of Lazarus's sister and of the Jews who are consoling her, "he groaned in the spirit, and was troubled"—in the presence, doubtless, of the reality of death and loss, of these consequences of the first act of disobedience that still constantly accompany us. He knows fear in anticipation of the cross and upon the cross. Like us, he knows temptation, and the author of Hebrews declares even that he "was in all points tempted" (Hebrews 4:15), as we are, without committing any sin, and that he thus is able to sympathize with our weaknesses. (That Jesus should have been tempted *in all points* as we are both gives us food for thought and reassures us.) Having died for our sins, he knows, while remaining perfectly innocent, what sin and guilt are.

And he knows our desire to find a path beyond sorrow, to discover a way of life that transcends our ever-threatened happiness. Not only does he teach an eminent and supernatural joy, but he seeks it for himself at the culminating moment of his life. According again to the Epistle to the Hebrews (12:2), if he "endured the cross, despising the shame," it was "for the joy that was set before him," that of sitting at the right hand of God.

Jesus lived in his person the triple fundamental experience that undergirds culture—all cultures. And is it not remarkable that Saint Paul ends his speech to the Athenians by affirming that God will judge the universe "by that man whom he hath ordained" and whom he has raised from the dead (Acts 17:31)? By a *man*: one might have worried over the insufficiency of the word, since Jesus was so much more than a simple mortal. But beyond the audacity in speaking of a man raised from the dead—a truly evangelical shock calculated to unsettle his listeners—does not Paul emphasize that salvation, which comes from on high and is decidedly not in our power, also passes through a unique man who is able to judge and save us because he knows intimately who we are? And this changes everything. The gospel is not above all a set of doctrines to which we must give our assent but the encounter, by the ear of faith, with a man, a God, and his saving life among us. It is the Son of God as a man, the Word incarnate, who understands, in their real sources, all our cultures, our intellectual enterprises, our organizations, our forms of behavior.

Christianity is in a favorable position to clarify the root experience that serves as a basis for culture, the feeling of an anguished contradiction between the two aspects of life—happiness and affliction—and the incessant, anxious quest for *something else*, for something beyond misfortune. For the Bible teaches, it seems to me, that such a motif is found at the heart of reality and that it appears in all domains. The conflict between what rejoices us and what distresses us is everywhere resolved in an unforeseeable and entirely superior joy. Christian anthropology proceeds from the original man created in the image and likeness of God to fallen and sinful man to man redeemed and glorified. The divine image, disfigured by the fall, is restored and transcended in the incarnation. History follows the same dynamic, advancing from the garden of Eden to a "cursed" soil (Genesis 3:17), then to the sublime garden called paradise. Cosmology goes from the creation of the heavens and the earth, of a whole which God declares to be "very good" (Genesis 1:31), to a universe subjected, on the other hand, to "vanity" and to "corruption" (Romans 8:20–21), awaiting a new creation at the end of time, "new heavens" and a "new earth" (Isaiah 65:17 and elsewhere). Even in its *theology*, its discourse on God, the Bible presents him as creator, judge, and savior.

It is not a motif to contemplate, in its elegance and complexity. Its ternary movement is existential as well as ontological: it engages us. It promises above all something new, in part for now. Biblical anthropology also treats the spiritual death of the "old man" and the birth of a "new man," which we must put on (Ephesians 4:22–24). Everything speaks of newness and hope, and touches the experience of us all, Christians or not, judging by the glimpses, in all forms of art and thought, of another splendor, of a renewed nature, of a self-transcendent humanity.

3.

If Christ incarnate knew, in our place and on our Earth, life, death, and resurrection, all Christians are invited to follow him in each one of these stages and to testify of this in the culture where they find themselves. Saint Paul goes so far as to write, "I live; yet not I, but Christ liveth in me" (Galatians 2:20). These words, which suggest a radically other point of view on anthropology, no doubt surpass our intelligence by evoking an experience far above ours. At least we thus know what perfection to aim at. Paul writes this as well, on the subject of Christ as the supreme goal of our life: "That I may know him, and the power of his resurrection, and the fellowship of his sufferings, being made conformable unto his death, if by any means I might attain unto the resurrection of the dead" (Philippians 3:10–11). Life, death-and-suffering, resurrection-and-power: the Christian is led to know at the deepest level happiness, sorrow, and hope—what could be more vital than the life of Christ, what more grievous than his death, more elating than his resurrection?— and can then demonstrate the manner in which this ternary vision is propagated in the culture and gives it form.

For in the most materialistic, the most secularized culture, the dynamic of dissatisfaction is at work. All the forms of art, far from constituting a simple entertainment, a pleasant supplement to the individual's and society's serious efforts, are found at the heart of our reflections on the human condition. If one distances oneself from mockery, from exhibitionism, from enchantment with success or the market—from all the temptations that naturally threaten enterprises that are, at their level, salutary—those forms give themselves to the search for a reality, a manner of being, beyond the polarity of happiness and sorrow. Dance transcends, during the performance, the vitality and mortality of the body and offers a glimpse of a free, creative, airborne body that recalls the Christian promise of a "glorious" and "spiritual" body. Music, which exists both in the ear and nowhere, transfigures the human voice, transforms the noises of the world into sounds, and gives to time—the medium of all our happinesses, which, however, leads us toward death—a new form, a tempo that makes of it a kind of temporary paradise. Painting, if it is somewhat figurative, renews our way of seeing, as well as a body, a tree, or several objects on a console that, in the elsewhere of the painting, constitute a presence perfectly and otherwise colored, drawn, given volume, and seen in a light of another order. By dint of saying what it observes, poetry also transforms it by welcoming it in sounds and rhythms, by articulating it anew in a syntax. The more faithful it remains, the more it changes it, so to speak, into itself, by imaginative figures and by an equally renewed language.

All the arts, including sculpture, architecture, photography, and cinema, project glimpses of a new humanity upon a new earth and under new skies. Even the most desperate, skeptical, atheistic work creates hope by its form, by its order or its knowing disorder. But these are, indeed, but hints that, while drawing us toward the possible and the better, confirm the incompleteness of our reality and leave us in our hunger. The Christian artist knows this better than any others, he who can present only glimpses of what he sees "in a glass, darkly" (1 Corinthians 13:12). He can at least open his art to this sense of something else that awaits in reality. He can create beauty, not by following conventional criteria, nor by seeking it directly, for it comes, like eloquence or humility, when one concentrates on the work to be made, the word to be created, or the action to be accomplished. And beauty, among the ideas that expose our finite world to the infinite—truth, justice, goodness—is the only one to strike our senses, to include our body. The Christian artist can evoke, especially through form—through the new and finished life of the work—joy, which is both a promise and, for Christians, curiously, a commandment. Jesus speaks in this way to his disciples: "These things have I spoken unto you, that my joy might remain in you, and that your joy might be full" (John 15:11). Paul writes to the Philippians, "Rejoice in the Lord always: and again I say, Rejoice" (Philippians 4:4). Such an artist awakens hope both by the quality of his work and by the new perspective he brings on the culture of his era.

Christianity furnishes the reason for culture and for the art that is found at its center in numerous forms. Culture is born of the banishment from Eden, from man's and the world's happy harmony, which we have no trouble imagining but which does not correspond to reality as we live it. It confronts the problems posed by the fall. Its ultimate aim is to find better solutions, both individual and collective, in the world as it goes and, in less reduced and simplified societies than ours that take into account a possible transcendence, to seek a divine world present in life and after death.

And Christ incarnate, as I have said, is the beating heart of culture, whether we are conscious of it or not. A series of declarations by Jesus in the Gospel of John—among which are "I am the bread of life" (John 6:35), "I am the light of the world" (John 8:12), "I am the resurrection" (John 11:25)—show that everything good we receive emanates from him, that everything good we contemplate leads us to him. One of these declarations—"I am the way, the truth, and the life" (John 14:6)—could even allude, along with its deeper meanings, if my suggestion is not too ingenious, to three great cultures or civilizations. The Way evokes China, the truth, Greece, and the life, Israel.

Since Christ is the Word made flesh, the Word that, in the beginning, spoke the universe into existence and that lived among us, looking through him we see the entire world in a different way. The universe is no longer indifferent, hostile, blind. It is endowed with a life that Hebrew poetry sings with metaphors that are undoubtedly more than a manner of speaking—very exact descriptions: "The heavens declare the glory of God, and the firmament sheweth his handywork" (Psalm 19:1); "Praise the Lord from the earth, ye dragons, and all deeps" (Psalm 148:7). Everything changes through this vision: "Behold," writes Paul, "all things are become new" (2 Corinthians 5:17). The expression recurs in Revelation and is accomplished in the new Creation at the end of time: "Behold, I make all things new" (Revelation 21:5). If we really think about it, the prevailing disquietude seems so great that our era could well be not the least but the most propitious for evangelization! *Now* is the favorable time, and at any rate, we have none other.

6

Art, the Strange Hope

1.

Let us examine this presence of art, its promises and its limits, in the light of hope.

The Bible, the book of hope and expectation, presents itself as a literary work. The Old Testament, which retraces Israel's hope in a creating and saving God and its expectation of the Messiah, develops in narratives often scattered with songs, in verse plays, Job and the Song of Songs, and in an abundance of poems, from the Psalms, Proverbs, and Lamentations to the visionary poetry of the prophets. The New Testament, which recounts the hope of Christians in a Son of God dead and risen and their expectation of his return, is vibrant with canticles, in the Gospel of Luke and Revelation, with hymns of the early church recorded in the epistles, with countless quotations of poetry in the Old Testament, and especially with the poems of Jesus, which enlarge the Gospels and culminate in the Lord's Prayer and the Beatitudes. Here is what should undergird our reflection. God revealed himself in large part in literary forms. The Holy Spirit very often inspired its writers by sharpening their artistic gifts.

The consequences of this presence of art in the revelation of salvation are numerous. In the very texts that teach us hope, art is not secondary or adventitious, is not an ornament one could do without. The power felt in the Revelation comes from the words that constitute its body. The form of a response to Jesus in the Gospel of Mark—"Lord, I believe; help thou mine unbelief" (Mark 9:24)— was not unrelated to my conversion. The paradox of a faith that is in reality a lack of faith, the audible and unfamiliar play between "believe" and "unbelief" (between *pisteuô* and *apistia* in Greek), the wavering, the conciseness of the phrase—everything contributed to astonishing me and seizing me and seemed to respond in a few words to my anguish. I doubt that the same sudden illumination would have reached me by reading the New English Bible ("I have faith . . . help me where faith falls short") or the Jerusalem Bible ("I believe! Come help my feeble faith!"), with their lack of penetrating exactness.

The translation of the Bible is also an art, and an art in the service of hope.

The art of the Scriptures partakes of our reception of their "message" and of our response to the God who inspired them. In the liturgy as well, language, song, instrumental music, like the architecture of the place, remain inseparable from worship, praise, thanksgiving, confession, and intercession. Aesthetic experience is based on spiritual experience. The pleasure of the ears and eyes represents a danger, quite obviously, if, by isolating it, we let it dominate all our attention. But Paul exhorts thus the Christians of Ephesus when they assemble: "Speaking to yourselves in psalms and hymns and spiritual songs, singing and making melody in your heart to the Lord" (Ephesians 5:19). (The sentence begins *laloúntes heautois*, speaking to one another, perhaps recalling the seraphim in Isaiah's vision who declare the holiness and the glory of God, where "one cried unto another," Isaiah 6:3.) The art of liturgy touches the heart, as the heart blossoms into poems and songs. The same recommendation to the Colossians: "Teaching and admonishing one another in psalms and hymns and spiritual songs, singing with grace in your hearts to the Lord" (Colossians 3:16). One senses behind Paul the centuries of exuberant Jewish worship. James encourages the solitary Christian in the same manner. If he suffers, he should pray, and "Is any merry? Let him sing psalms" (James 5:13).

As for Christian art, which spreads beyond the Bible in all possible forms, Jacques Maritain has undoubtedly said what is essential in his book *Art and Scholasticism*: "If you want to make a Christian work, then *be* Christian, then simply try to make a beautiful work, into which your heart will pass; do not try to 'make Christian.'"[1] Art becomes thus a testimony, the tangible presence of a Christian vision of things, and a way of responding to Peter's injunction to "be ready always to give an answer to every man that asketh you a reason of the hope that is in you" (1 Peter 3:15). Christian art will consciously do in its own manner everything that non-Christian art does, and when I pray for the poem I am preparing to write—or that I am working on or that I think finished—to be true, I expect the beauty to blossom in the truth inscribed in the real, independent of us, of which Jesus is, in the final analysis, the guide and the incarnation.

---

1   Jacques Maritain, *Art and Scholasticism and the Frontiers of Poetry*, trans. Joseph W. Evans (South Bend, IN: University of Notre Dame Press, 1974), 66.

2.

Remarkably, humanity needs, everywhere and always, to create art. Something moves us to pass through forms in order to see better, to dream of somewhere else, to recognize ourselves, to penetrate into what transcends us, with the hope of understanding a reality whose reason eludes us. In the anxious conviction, it seems, that we are lacking a key.

Everything plays out in the irresistible joy of form. And that is true, whether it is a comical drawing or a tragedy that is concerned. Colors on a canvas, volumes extracted from rock, body movements dancing improbably, almost gloriously, chords or perfectly arranged dissonances in an unexpected invisible, words that speak to each other and resound in the new language of the poem, a narrative, an action that is born and, whatever the horror that it produces, resolves itself in a consummate integrity: this art, this articulation has the singular power to bring us out of ourselves into a world apparently gorged with being and better ordered than the one we inhabit. Art surprises us, as much as a landscape transformed by a streak of lightning, as soon as we pay attention to it.

This surprise, precious, leads us to be surprised by the familiar world. Art—whether it be, let us say, pagan, atheistic, or indifferent—possesses this virtue of proposing to us in the accustomed, the bizarre, in the known, something else. Not only the landscapes of the Christian Constable, for example, but the Egyptian colossal, the singular sonorities of the late Beethoven, even the simple complexity of an ode by Horace open us to what transcends the real such as we perceive it and lift us above ourselves. Paradoxically, great art makes us very small, unworthy of its soaring flight, while giving us the impression of growing inordinately, of finding ourselves inhabiting a more elevated region.

Any work of art, if it distances us from our familiar space, also frees us from duration. Claudel describes, in "La Poésie est un art" (Poetry is an art), the effect produced by a line from Virgil's *Georgics* (book 1, line 496): "The moment by the magic of art is endowed with eternity." Curiously, the line, which Claudel quotes (and not quite accurately) as "Et gravibus rostris galeas pulsavit inanes," seems unrelated to such an ambition. After the barbarism of civil war, the farmer "will, with his heavy hoe, strike on hollow helmets." Reading the line as a poet, Claudel understands that this concentration on objects and on the brusque contact with matter creates a very rich mental world, and that the effort to pronounce these consonants and vowels that, in being repeated, transmit to us the farmer's effort is precisely what permits us to gain access to this world. One hears, he writes, the hollow sound of the impact "like memory"; it is we who are plowing "the field of the past" and who are causing "these accusing fragments." The peasant's surprise, the Latin poet's indignation, and this sudden discovery of a forgotten evil situate the event in the atemporal milieu of the spirit.

It is true that in poetry, as in the novel, certain passages seem particularly apt to project us beyond time. However, any literary text in its entirety produces a *tempo* that is foreign to our biological and natural time, which is uncontrollable, and offers a glimpse, if not of eternity, of an absence of time or a time that is other. From the beginning right to the end, and without ceasing to explore earthly realities, the *Georgics* exist otherly.

I return to Claudel's sentence, whose prose also situates us beyond time. It could have succeeded in doing this, but in a rather unremarkable manner, by following the normal and, so to speak, regular word order: "The moment is endowed with eternity by the magic of art," or "By the magic of art, the moment is endowed with eternity." The completeness of the syntax would have already sufficed to isolate it in a verbal world. The Claudelian transposition—"The moment by the magic of art is endowed with eternity"—follows its own tempo by the more marked rhythm and the slightly strange order of words and arouses the hope, if one attends carefully to it, of a new, perfected language. Behind this language, behind this pale reflection of the Word, there is profiled an equally better world.

The vision, procured by art, of a new space and an extraordinary tempo—of another *place*—strikes us in a great cathedral or a little Romanesque church. Whether or not we are Christians, it seems to us, during our visit and perhaps beyond, that there must exist somewhere a world that responds to this aspiration and this reverence. And the stones erected—menhirs, dolmens, cromlechs, with their troubling names and their lost neolithic origin—are just as impressive. Truer than the too-human representations of gods, they reveal, in a sense, nothing, but this nothing is the secret of their mystery. Their massive presence, whether solitary or multiple and obscurely organized, with their art that we hardly understand, shows us, by stopping us in our tracks, that despite the profusion of our knowledge, we do not know the world that we inhabit and that there are other things. Those superhuman stones introduce us, with an enigmatic authority, into the domain of the strange.

3.

And the strange is the domain of hope. Hope clings to an unknown beyond all the known, to a peace, a joy beyond the happiness and the sorrow of ordinary existence. The erected stones, like the Egyptian sphinxes or the moai on Easter Island, suggest the strange in a particularly powerful way and better than the sacred art of the Greeks, in that their authors seem to admit that their intuition exceeds their knowledge and that they are incapable of naming what they are divining. They also lead us to think that art does not necessarily seek beauty, or that that is not their essential goal. We do not understand it either, despite centuries of affirmations about it. It does not let itself be pinned down by the diverse abstractions that we interpose: harmony, proportion, and others. I even wonder if the seventeenth-century classicists were not inspired to evoke a *je ne sais quoi* present, but undefinable, in the great works. For beauty transports us beyond the work, beyond familiar reality toward a hoped-for peace, toward a possible joy. But Carnac and the great sphinx of Giza produce the same effect. *Je ne sais quoi*, an antiquated expression, excessively repeated and obviously vague, translates with exactness our *unknowing* of what calls out to us in art and of the alterity toward which art leads us.

The Bible is not much interested in the beauty of art. The New Testament only mentions some sepulchers whose outward appearance is beautiful (Matthew 23:27) and the Gate Beautiful of the temple (Acts 3:2, 10). For the Bible explores another phenomenon that transcends us even more: glory. If glory is, at the source, something like the radiance of the Godhead, it is also the splendor that conceals him. We only know, thanks to Psalm 24, that God is "the King of glory" and, thanks to the Acts of the Apostles, that he reveals himself such as Stephen saw him at the moment of his martyrdom: he "saw the glory of God" (Acts 7:55). This celestial glory stretches, far more than beauty, over all creation. We know this by the seraphim's cry in Isaiah's presence: "Holy, holy, holy is the Lord of hosts: the whole earth is full of his glory" (Isaiah 6:3). The author's vow in Psalm 72 expresses the same idea from the point of view of humans living on a fallen earth: "Blessed be his glorious name for ever: and let the whole earth be filled with his glory!" (Psalm 72:19). When we look at the universe, the creation of God and the supreme work of art, we see also, according to the passionate *attack* of Psalm 19, that "the heavens declare the glory of God." Glory reigns everywhere, visible even if we do not see it, but what it *is* eludes us, and must without any doubt elude us. As the immensity of the night sky offers a little sign, perceptible, of the dimensions of God's being, glory seems to suggest—but we are out of our depth here—his ineffable light. It is thus that God is God, marvelously present, inaccessible to our theology. In explaining Christ's resurrection, Paul places it outside the reach of our explanations: "Christ was raised up from the dead by the glory of the Father" (Romans 6:4). And how does the Old Testament speak of the beauty of art? "Lord, I have loved the habitation [rendered 'beauty' in the Jerusalem Bible in French] of thy house, and the place where thine honor [also rendered 'glory'] dwelleth" (Psalm 26:8). The beauty of the tabernacle has the function of rendering discernible to the heart, not the beauty of God, but his transcendent glory.

4.

Art in general, whether or not it knows the Christian God, awakens, by its elusive beauty or its troubling mystery, the hope of a world that is other. It gives birth, with clarity and by its simple mode of existence, to the hope of change. Everything is changed in a work of art. To speak of the art that I know by practicing it, that of the poem, naming the real with words in a certain arrangement, with sounds and studied rhythms of which readers become conscious, is enough to change them, to make resonate that which was probably silent: a lamp, a lock of hair, a sentiment, a memory, an idea. The work of the poem consists in creating an original place where the real presents itself in a new light. Probed and formed by a language altogether self-conscious and also altogether well oriented toward what it is discovering, even the common emotions, even the known ideas, take on an unaccustomed body and contours. The sense of a strange place asserts itself especially in poetry in verse. The end of each line, with the interruption and the reinforcement of rhythm, like the aspect of a piece of writing that avoids prose, situates the poem in an elsewhere, where anything can happen. In following a newly shaped syntax, words dialoguing with each other, presences of the real and elements of the lived brought together thus for the first time, one appreciates the change brought to the world, or more precisely to our fashion of seeing it. A renewed vision and language give a view of hope, of the world and its possibilities.

Painting also is hope, whatever the object of its regard. A river in a painting proves quite inferior to a real river: no fish can smell its freshness, no wind can ruffle its surface. It is nonetheless superior in its own way: it flows without flowing, the light that animates it is enriched with another kind of life, the colors that compose it correspond to a particular sensibility and obey a necessity whereof nature has no knowledge. One glimpses in a painted landscape another land. And in what world are we to imagine, in painting, objects so banal as a knife, an apple on a plate? What peace—but where? still to come?—breathes in a still life![2] Then, the surest indication of the intrinsic capacity of art to change everything it touches is photography. Far from reproducing the visible by a mechanical, objective, and perfectly exact gaze, it composes it, by the choice of an angle and of a frame; it brings to it a seed and one would almost say a touch all its own; it gives it a *meaning* that originates in the photographer's eye. It transposes the visible into a photo; it modifies our way of seeing; it causes a world to shimmer—especially perhaps in black-and-white photos—strangely changed.

This change effected continually by art, this desire of a world transformed, must one not associate them with the biblical promise of "new heavens" and a "new earth?" This promise—made by God himself in Isaiah's prophecy (65:17), passed on by Peter in his second epistle (3:13), held forth in John's vision in Revelation (21:1),

---

2 The French term for "still life," *nature morte*, literally means "dead nature," so there is a bit of word-play here.

but often neglected in Christian circles—describes, with images at once precise and purely suggestive, paradise, the place of life after death. All forms of art seem to strain toward the new earth, whatever might be the thought of the artist. The living presence of the work aspires to this renewal and constitutes its image, rather weak but how alluring. Could one also think that the work of the artist constitutes a very distant reflection of the work of the universe, which also seeks to be transformed? According to Paul, creation is in "earnest expectation" of the end, with the "hope" of being delivered from corruption: "The whole creation groaneth and travaileth in pain together" (Romans 8:19–22). We live in a vast material domain that is hoping and endeavoring to change; our art is the echo, on our level, of this immense aspiration.

5.

Art does not necessarily signify hope by what it shows, says, or makes heard, by its sometimes wretched "content"; it brings hope in itself, in its manner of being. There is nothing to compare with this intimate hope of the work to convince us that art does not exist by chance but that it reveals God's providence, that it is a gift of God and a sign of the new creation to come. Yet art indeed only constitutes a sign, and the hope it offers resembles only from afar that of Christianity. It unveils for us the stunning strangeness of the world, being potentially capable of leading us toward the stunning strangeness of the gospel. But alone, it is not sufficient. One must not confuse its atemporal aspect with eternity nor its aesthetic delight with prayer. If it evokes the transcendent, the sacred, the numinous, it leads just as well to a Buddha as to the God of glory. It can awaken a worldly hope—by the endurance of suffering in the characters of a novel or play, for example—but not a Christian hope.

The limited role of art is explained in that it can attain beauty, if such is the desire and capacity of the artist, but not that which seems to stand beyond beauty: glory. We would do well to meditate again on Isaiah's declaration about the Messiah as Suffering Servant: "He hath no form nor comeliness; and when we shall see him, there is no beauty that we should desire him" (Isaiah 53:2). "No beauty": perhaps we have not truly assimilated this very curious expression. He who *is* our hope (1 Timothy 1:1) does not appear in a form that art comprehends. Like Christianity, Jesus is different and radiates from himself, not beauty, but the "glory" of God, of whom he is the "brightness" (Hebrews 1:3). Glory too is a *je ne sais quoi* that eludes us and transcends art. Even the art of the Bible, which names it, does not have the mission of showing it to us.

The power of art vanishes as soon as we think of true hope. We hope "for that we see not" (Romans 8:25), and for that, we need not art but faith. According to the always stunning affirmation of the Epistle to the Hebrews, faith is "the substance of things hoped for, the evidence of things not seen" (Hebrews 11:1). Art creates hope for the life that ends in death, but not the foolish hope revealed by the Bible, which is founded on the resurrection from the dead (1 Corinthians 15:19–20). To return to the word that energizes this discussion, Christ within us is "the hope of glory" (Colossians 1:27), and we are living "in hope of the glory of God" (Romans 5:2).

Yet we are also haunted by the idea that art surpasses life because it is more living, more colorful, more real. The idea becomes irresistible when, while listening to a great piece of music, we wonder why, between joy and sadness, we don't have access to the more highly cerebral and sensual world that it evokes. Good question, indeed, since the perfection of art suggests that reality *is not going well*, being, as Christianity affirms, fallen. But art could serve as an ersatz of life, an idol that attracts us and distances us from the only world where hope dwells. Constable's position seems just as necessary:

"Nothing can surpass the beauty of the countryside; by comparison, paintings are trash." To be torn in our admiration between the countryside and the painting is doubtless an advantage for us, as it is salutary for the Christian to aspire to paradise while loving the creation and the earthly life where God has placed them. After having attracted us, art must lead us toward the everyday real where hope is active. Art represents both a threshold into something other and a door opening onto the present of the considerably enriched world. And *the* great work of art is certainly creation, which God even found "good"—*tov* in the Hebrew of Genesis, *kalos* in the Septuagint's version. A living presence right down to inorganic matter, creation reveals its creator. According to the already cited Psalm 19, the heavens declare his "glory" and the firmament "sheweth forth his handywork" (Psalms 19:1). Beyond the beauty of nature and the aesthetic experience that it provides us, this unfathomable *glory* inspires in us a more profound sentiment that takes hold of our entire being: reverential fear, fright mixed with respect, what in English we call "awe." This is even the first sentiment, it seems, that the Bible attributes to him who contemplates creation: the earth, the daytime sky—smiling or dangerous—the unlimited sky of night. For "that which may be known of God" by looking around ourselves, what "is clearly seen, being understood by the things that are made," is not his love or his mercy but first of all, according to Paul, his unthinkable transcendence, "his eternal power and Godhead" (Romans 1:19–20).

One would say that for Paul, to proclaim the "testimony of God" should produce in his hearers the same reverential fear. His preaching in Corinth was "a demonstration of the Spirit and of power," and he presented himself as "in weakness and in fear and in much trembling" (1 Corinthians 2:1–4).

We thus distance ourselves from human art in order to find a more efficacious source for hope. However, am I right in thinking that we all know moments when, in the presence of a misty valley, a garden plot, or even an old wall, we get the impression that something is happening, that the visible is seized with a strange perfection, with a sudden depth of being? As if nature, more real, withdrew into itself and waited to be able to reveal itself in its true reality, both the same and other. The object of our gaze strangely resembles, at those moments, a work of art, a painting conceived and executed in a miraculous way. It reveals to us what we *see* in true paintings, in poetic "descriptions": glimpses of the unimaginable work to be accomplished in the "new heavens" and the "new earth."

7

The Charitable Work
of Translation

1.

The Bible is the absolute book of hope, as all Scripture is inspired, according to Saint Paul (2 Timothy 3:16), and for Christians who hear it as the word of God. But very few Christians read the Bible in Hebrew and Greek; they are obliged to get to know it in translation. Since the translations are not inspired, whatever the piety of the translators or the help God brings them, must we conclude that we always find ourselves confronted with a word that is less reliable and necessarily diminished?

The Catholic Church avoided the question for a long time by assuming that the Vulgate was just as authoritative as the Bible. Consequently, others translating into the vulgar languages thought it natural to translate, not the Bible, but the Vulgate. The Port-Royal Bible, for example, and the English Bible by Wycliffe and his collaborators are translations of a translation. As if, to give a version

of Sophocles in English, one based it on a German translation. All
this confusion served only to hide the problem.

What is at stake in translation, quite grave in the case of the Bible,
is important and instructive in secular translations. All translation,
read or undertaken, places us before the multiplicity of languages
and before the fact that each language constitutes a perspective on
the real and on the self, as well as a way of thinking. To learn a
foreign language, for him who really pays attention to it, is to enter
into a new world, to recognize that there exist many others, and to
look with an amazed eye at the world that one has always inhabited
and that one considered unique. Such an apprenticeship—perhaps
the most precious we can offer a student—possesses a profoundly
moral dimension: it brings us out of ourselves and lets us feel the
intelligence and the sensibility of another. It can even have a spir-
itual dimension according to the religious definition of the word:
whatever comes from the Holy Spirit is spiritual, if ever this ini-
tiation to the strange—to the strangeness of all that is implied
in a foreign language and to the strangeness of all that was once
familiar—is transformed into the intuition of another alterity, of
another presence among customary things.

This profusion of languages can also be worrisome. But
must we conclude, along with a whole section of modern French
thought, that language does not give us access to the real? By add-
ing to the arbitrariness of the sign according to Saussure the almost
equally famous declaration by Mallarmé—"Languages imperfect
through being several, the supreme one is lacking"—must we
believe that the diversity of idioms prohibits us from finding the
truth? In a sense, yes. The Christian knows that he inhabits a fallen
world, that he himself is the most obvious indication of it, and
that language participates in that fall. Each language comes short
of what it names; we seek the path in the chiaroscuro of a real-
ity excluded from Eden. From this angle, Babel is decidedly a

punishment. However, the limits of our competence do not mean that the only reality is that produced by our words; that beyond our stammerings, reality only exists in our wishful imagination as a sort of dream; that the only thing that counts is our capacity to create—from the kaleidoscope of several thousand languages—a common world upon which we can agree. For the Christian, God's presence guarantees the existence of an objective reality independent of our discourse and of our will. Even those for whom God is a useless hypothesis must feel the resistance of reality, which rejects formula after formula when they seek to express it, a resistance that one discovers quite clearly in the poetic act, where attention becomes particularly rigorous and complex.

It would be sad to lose this experience of reality living its own life, of a transcendence in the philosophical sense of the term—that of the world in relation to conscience—capable of serving as a doorway to the religious sense, to God's transcendence. The author of Genesis, recounting how God gave to Adam the task of naming certain of his creatures, lets us suppose that the first man was able to do that because he understood perfectly—at his own level, that of a creature made in God's image—the very being of those other creatures, and that in giving them names and establishing a relationship with them, he adds something to creation: he institutes a human perspective on reality that modifies it, according to the truth of the creatures issued from God and according to the truth of man. We no longer have as clear and pure a vision as Adam, but we still seek to name the real; we do this necessarily on the basis of what we are, and we have at our disposition numerous possibilities offered by the multiplicity of our languages. As it is said in a poem by Kevin Hart, "The rain complete[s] its work inside our words."[1]

---

1   Kevin Hart, "Little Songbook of the Dark One," in *Barefoot* (South Bend, IN: Notre Dame University Press, 2018), 19.

All the arts open us to this other transcendence that surpasses the real as we perceive it. The one I know best, poetry, so present in the Bible, troubles the real by the sounds and syntactic and semantic networks into which it invites it and permits us, by its singular forms, to see ourselves in a different way and to catch in the familiar world a glimpse of something else. Poetry, even in its lightest expressions, is a serious business. To write poems is to accept a great responsibility. For the poem is not content to exist. It constitutes rather an *energeia*, an energy, an active force that never ceases to operate. It is often said that a poem, a novel, a play does not exist in itself, that it needs readers, directors, actors in order for the sleeping text to awake. Which gives many the impression of exercising a considerable power: "Without us, Corneille would be a dead letter." I would say rather that the work is never completed, that it works in all those who engage themselves thoroughly in it, and that it changes a lot or a little according to the new perspectives one brings to it, generation after generation. The work also works through the translations in which it is diversified, and there, in particular, it changes.

If the original poem is present in a different way in a translation, the translation too changes the real, in the ways the new language behaves. The translator also is responsible, and doubly so, before the real and before the poem of which he dares give his own version. For the translation of a poem changes the poem. We know this, but without discerning what results from it. As poetry participates in the possible of the world, translation participates in the possible of poetry. Translation is not a last resort, a regrettable but necessary ersatz: it is the next step. I would gladly speak of *the poetic work of translation*, creative and transformative, and of the *setting in translation* of a poem in the same way we speak of its setting in music. This presumes that one does not prepare to translate a great poem, which emerges from the depths of a language and from the intense intellectual and affective work implied, by importing exclusively into one's own language the meaning, the surface, as if the translator did not have to effectuate the same work as the poet. Translation is an act of writing and a *poièsis*.

But the drama is that translators, often eminent specialists, generally have no mastery of their own language. They do not even seem to ask themselves the question, imagining doubtless that it is enough to be immersed into a language from infancy in order to know it. This absence of knowledge, this incapacity to inhabit all the remote corners of one's language, this ignorance of its resources and the proper means of augmenting them, explains why good translations are so rare.

We must take all these questions into consideration in order to reflect seriously on what is at stake in the translation of the Bible.

2.

And what is happening in the act of translating? "Act," indeed, as one says "poetic act," for the translator is engaged in a process just as complex as that of the poet and in an almost equally exacting act of making. (I am concentrating on poetry because in it the requirements of translation are the most stringent and the most obvious. It is concerning the poetry of the Bible that the problem of biblical translation culminates.) The translator finds himself facing a multiple alterity, which he does not simply note (as those who only reflect on translation) but progressively discovers. He discovers the other language, not in general, but in the life it leads in the growing strangeness of a poem with innumerable secrets. He discovers the different real from which the poem has emerged and that the poem brings into existence in a new form. He discovers another who is not exactly the poet with whom he could converse in a café but rather the conscience and the unconscious that the poem have created, or that have created themselves, thanks to the elaboration of the poem. He discovers the human being the poet himself had discovered in writing. If this being is in some way fictional, he nevertheless evokes the poet in body and spirit who assumes him and to whom the translator is accountable. As the latter feels little by little the radical transcendence of a foreign language, he feels the remote strangeness of this other who fascinates him, and this encounter with what is not himself can mutate, in the very act of the work, into a more solemn encounter, into the intuition of a true transcendence.

It is also to be hoped that the translator *discovers* his own language, in each effort to say anew and in a different way a given word, a given grammatical structure, a given rhythm, a given cluster of sounds.

Serious translation develops also, verse by verse, word by word, syllable by syllable, like an act of reading. It constitutes perhaps the best way to read a poem, the most penetrating and, at bottom, because of the good translator's persistence, the most faithful.

And if the original poem is an energy, a force that operates in its readers, the poem the translator composes is as well, as long as he takes his act in full seriousness. The ideal would be for the translator of the work of a great poet to be a great poet himself; this is obvious when one thinks about it, but we tend to forget it. Since this ideal rarely takes place in reality, what can one reasonably ask of the translator of Petrarch, of Whitman, of Neruda? In his *Salon de 1859*, Baudelaire, thinking of the way certain artists "translate" poetic works, declares, with a perfectly justified severity, that it "is not permissible to translate poets except when one feels within oneself an energy equal to theirs." For translation in the ordinary sense of the word, it is equally true that not only are a great knowledge of the other language, a tenacity, and an ample capacity for work necessary but above all an energy, an unstinting ardor for imagining, inventing, probing the real and the self, putting one's language and oneself into motion, expanding the possible. Translation is an activity that is partly, and very seriously, moral, and Baudelaire proposes that one examine oneself before undertaking it. If the result is disappointing, one is not *permitted* to continue.

And since the translation of a poem is a poem, the translator needs not translatology, not some theory of translation, but his own poetic resources. He learns as well, by scrutinizing as an artist the foreign language he is preparing to serve, how false and dangerous it is to speak of the mastery of a language. A language is a more complex structure than our speech, a music that exceeds our song, an untamable beast. Of one's own language one is also the student, even if, by cooperating with it, one succeeds in proposing some innovation to it. And a translator depends—just as much as poets before the blank page and their desire for a poem, and in the tangle that generally is the gestation of a translation as of a poem—on ideas, on turns of phrase, on cadences, on sonorities that come from we know not where, or do not come. The translator can grasp, just as well as the poet, how good it is to be dependent and that this dependence brings freedom and creativity.

3.

This long detour through poetry and translation in general was necessary in order better to understand, by considering it from a new angle, the translation of the Bible. I have emphasized in my book *Bible et poésie* that the necessity of translating the Bible must have been foreseen in the process by which God was going to reveal himself "to the nations," that it was not a small detail forgotten through inattention. This providence will help us approach, later, the problem that I raised at the beginning of this chapter, that of the difference between the Bible and its translations. For the moment, let us concentrate on the translator while recognizing that translating the Bible is a great privilege, one that the translator does not always seem to think about, and above all a fearsome responsibility. In this context, we could reprise Baudelaire's warning, adapting it as follows: it is not permissible to translate the psalms of David unless one feels within oneself an energy equal to his. Can we be sure that the translators of the Psalms, of the book of Job, of the Song of Songs, and so on, in the numerous modern versions of the Bible have found in themselves such an energy, or even that they sought it? It is equally in relation to literature in general that Baudelaire maintains that there is "in the word, in the *Word*, something *sacred* that prohibits us from making of it a game of chance." How much more important is this warning for whoever is about to trouble the language of God's word, knowing that that word gives access to the Word! Biblical translators find themselves in a demanding moral situation, facing permissions to solicit and prohibitions not to neglect.

The translator of Goethe is committed—should be committed—to showing that Goethe is a great poet and not, if the translation is mediocre, a great man expressing himself clumsily. Bible translators accept—should accept—the obligation to show in their own idiom that the Bible is the book of books, the word of God. They must turn their pens seven times in their hand before writing. Beyond the energy of David, Isaiah, Matthew, Paul, is found the energy of the Holy Spirit, of the living God. Translation must let this energy, this active and other language, pass through; it cannot do this unless the translator, not being content to communicate with exactness a "message," understands the immense talent being asked of him. He examines, he tries to hear, not only often difficult texts contained in numerous manuscripts, but a language that is only partly of this world, because it comes—via the intimate experience, the listening, and the diligence of human authors—from God. He encounters these other selves, produced finally, in this knowable form, by their writings, which take him out of himself and which he must mime in order to understand them. He encounters God above all and an immense world that is liable nevertheless, by its apparent familiarity after two millennia of preaching and of exegesis, to lose its troubling and joyous strangeness. Paul affirms that we see by our intelligence, in the visible world, the invisible of God, "his eternal power and Godhead" (Romans 1:20). Does one not also sense in the Bible that same power and that same Godhead? What we see in creation, we hear in the Scriptures.

I see very well that this kind of comparison could be illegitimate, since the Bible does not make it. But the *other* power of the Bible is certain, and the translator must accept the obligation to transmit it. The Bible is profoundly foreign to us, like the revelation it gives and imposes and the faith it offers and commands. The translator is not required—as was claimed, quite casually and ignorantly, in a press release for the *Revised English Bible*—to make it "accessible," "available for today's reader." As if, in producing a Bible that is easy to read, one did not deprive the reader of its richness and of its mystery. We immediately grasp what we would lose in providing more accessible versions of Shakespeare or of Racine; why do we not see the danger of a similar treatment of the Bible?

4.

The opposite of an easy-to-read biblical translation is assuredly not a translation that is difficult to read. The translator is invited to show what he finds, simple or complex, limpid or mysterious, to allow to pass into his own language the power of the original, thanks to an appropriate language. But how to find this language if one is not a writer? And should we not be surprised by the fact that most modern translators of the Bible are not? Those of the Bible de Port-Royal and the King James Bible, as well as Tyndale,

Coverdale, Luther, while possessing the requisite linguistic and theo-
logical knowledge, were true writers and understood well that the
literary resources at their disposal were indispensable. Without
those, how could the Bible strike the mind and touch the heart?
But here is how the translators of the New English Bible reasoned
in 1970, with a stupefying naïveté and a carelessness disguised as
wisdom and modesty: "Apprehending, however, that sound schol-
arship does not necessarily carry with it a delicate sense of English
style, the committee appointed a fourth panel, of trusted literary
advisors." If they recognized that they did not have the gift of
writing, why did they agree to translate the Bible? One cannot
imagine a specialist in Russian saying, "As a great Tolstoy scholar,
I have translated *War and Peace*, but, not being a writer, I asked
a novelist to revise my text and improve the style." Knowing that
one has no sense of rhythm, that one does not instinctively hear
the sounds of language, that one does not know how to listen to the
memory and the intimate life of words and the dialogues they
establish among themselves, must one not abstain?

One could object that the Bible is not literature. In a sense, this
is correct. We must not read it as we read Balzac or Valéry. How-
ever, the Bible, which is other-than-literature, is nevertheless a set
of writings. As revelation, it transcends literature, as it transcends
everything human, but God often chooses as witnesses, as writers
of his word, poets, storytellers, playwrights. Everywhere, thought
and emotion are formed by the very manner in which they become
language. It is disappointing to read translations that do not seem
to take note of this, thereby weakening the Bible.

One could say this in other ways: numerous modern translators
of the Bible are not translators; or, specialists in Hebrew or in clas-
sical Greek and the *koinè* of the New Testament, they are not spe-
cialists in their own language and have never thought it necessary
to be such. A translator thinks about complex questions inevitably

posed by translation: for example, must one erase all traces of the strangeness, the foreignness of the work, and leave one's own language in the state in which one finds it or, on the contrary, allow the reader to discern the foreign nature of the work that comes from a different culture through modifications that one brings to one's language? I do not presume to have the answer to that question; I simply think Bible translators should ask it.

The lack of knowledge of their own language leads some translators to impose chores on themselves with a distressing amateurism. Those of the New English Bible were seeking, according to the prefaces, "a contemporary idiom," "the current speech of our own time," "the English of the present day, that is . . . the natural vocabulary, constructions, and rhythms of contemporary speech."

Confusing a certain manner of speech with the energetic, supple, profound, varied, surprising English that writers find. Forgetting, or not noticing, that the translations of Tyndale or the King James are happily distanced from the everyday English of their eras. The idea of "a natural English" is a pipe dream, as would be that of a natural French; their pursuit in the first place of exactness and "clarity," with the "aim of making the meaning as clear as it could be made," makes clarity a fetish. They wish to offer untrammeled "the truth of the scriptures"; they should have understood that such a truth does not always manifest itself in a luminous language. The translators of the Revised English Bible desired everywhere "a fluent and idiomatic way of expressing," as if one could reduce the innumerable ways of constructing sentences and creating "style" into only one, and as if they wished the reader to assimilate the biblical texts with a minimum of effort.

Not knowing English, they nonetheless had the mad desire to translate the Bible into English. By reading their always poor and uncertain "style," one would not guess that the Bible is the word of the God of heaven and earth. In the third of his essays *On Epitaphs*,

Wordsworth evokes "those expressions which are not what the garb is to the body but what the body is to the soul, themselves a constituent part and power or function in the thought." The weakness in writing among biblical translators ignorant of this unity of thought and word, a unity that one can only achieve with labor and stubbornness and that is impossible to attain without a little talent, should provoke a profound anger—like that, moreover, of the new Anglican liturgies, replacements for an old liturgy that also *spoke*, that was penetrating and memorable.

5.

In order to speak of the principles of biblical translation, I have concentrated on English examples—I could have added some American examples that are just as troubling—because the language in which the most impressive series of translations of the Bible has been produced is the one that has recently suffered from a plethora of inadequate translations. This failure in the transmission of God's word—unpreparedness to write, errors in the translator's task—leads me to pose again the even more fundamental question with which I began. Since the translations are not the Bible itself, properly speaking, and are not inspired in the same way it is, are they of necessity muting the divine word?

Think of Babel. The story of the confusion of languages and the dispersion of peoples (Genesis 11:1–9) describes a punishment for the pride of the builders of the tower by which they wished to "reach unto heaven," a punishment we must not forget in our enthusiasm for the multiplicity of languages. Not speaking a single language separates us from each other; the fall of language, which followed the fall of man as a second effect of the same cause—inordinate pride—means, as I have said, that even in our native tongue, we do not have easy, immediate, and perfect access to the real. But the love of God blesses the consequences of his curses. The fall of man has made possible both the good and the evil of history, of culture; the multiplicity of languages has produced an abundance of visions of the world and of verbal musics. The profusion of languages even corresponds, curiously, to what God wished for all living beings according to the first commandment: "Be fruitful and multiply" (Genesis 1:22; 28). Multiplicity is just as much a source of joy as unity: multiplicity of creation, multiplicity of the Bible (with plurality of Gospels); unity of the universe, unity of God's word. The same phenomenon in the arts. As Schiller writes, "A sovereign unity is necessary [for the work of art], but it must not detract from diversity." (That unity may *detract* from diversity calls for reflection.) Pentecost, the response to Babel—just as the saving work of Christ, the "second" man, responds to the devastating sin of Adam, the "first" (1 Corinthians 15:45–47)—confirms the importance and mystery of multiplicity. "Men out of every nation under heaven" (Acts 2:5) hear in their own language what the disciples are saying. The disciples' native language is Aramaic, but under the Holy Spirit's inspiration, they speak "with other tongues" (Acts 2:4). And what do the disciples say? They publish "the wonderful works of God" (Acts 2:11). Would it be admissible to see in this miracle that renders the inspired praise of God audible—according to a motivated and pedagogical exaggeration—to all the peoples of the world an image of the future profusion of translations opening the word of God, proffered only in Hebrew up to that point, to all the languages of the planet? And the promise—dare we think it?—that the Holy Spirit will not remain indifferent to those translations? The Christian knows, after all, that even in a mediocre translation, God speaks to him. He approaches us in *our* words, in *our* syntax, which penetrates into our representation of the real and into our most intimate experience.

Yes, but are not Hebrew and Greek just as fallen as the other languages? Calling them "sacred languages" because God chose them to bring his revelation veils the difficulty to be resolved. If each language falls short of what it names, must we resign ourselves to finding in the Bible an imperfection, that of human language, and in the translations an even greater deficiency because of the absence of a seamless inspiration? Or can one assume, regarding the original, that God has revealed to us, of his transcendence, what we are capable of receiving and that Hebrew and Greek were apt to bear it? As for translations, if they disturb the biblical revelation, can one believe that in modifying it according to the characteristics of the translator's language, they develop it in order to make it enter into the ways of thinking and feeling in that language? Just as God has given us the Bible, he has given us languages, and he has given us translation, the ability to pass from one language to another. Can one go further? The French translation of a poem by Lorca, as long as it is excellent, offers a new life to the original, another way of being, of seeing, of singing and dancing that Spanish does not have. Can an excellent translation of the Bible, by rewriting it in the mind and matter of another language, offer other perspectives that do not affect the essential—the content of faith and the way of salvation—but are able to make the original live in a different way?

Take the example of a single word. The Greek for one of Paul's expressions that I have quoted several times—"Hè te aidios autou dunamis kai theiotès" (Romans 1:20)—becomes in Tyndale's New Testament and then in the King James "his eternal power and Godhead." The compound word *Godhead,* a very Germanic word inherited from the Anglo-Saxons, sounds differently for an English speaker from *theiotès* for a Greek or *divinité* for a French speaker; buttressed by the strength of the word *power* in the ear, it makes one shiver. A sentence that I have quoted elsewhere is transformed, in the translation of the French Jerusalem Bible—"Arrêtez, connaissez que moi je suis Dieu" (Psalm 46:11)—in a series of words issued from Latin. It is carried by the memory of that language, which gives

it a particular flavor. The King James Version of the English Bible—
"Be still, and know that I am God"—rewrites the original from the
depths of English: its Germanic origin, the genius of its monosylla-
bles, the slow gravity of which it is capable. The new rhythm affords
a new meaning to the Hebrew. As everywhere, translation opens an
unexpected window onto the original.

I hesitate to say it, but even a translation that falls involuntarily
a bit wide of the mark, while being rigorously thought out, can
become enlightening. In the course of his long prayer in chapter 17
of the Gospel of John, Jesus affirms that of the disciples his Father
has given him, "none of them is lost, but *ho huios tès apôleios*" (John
17:12). The French Jerusalem Bible and Segond Bible translate it as
"the son of perdition" (the literal meaning), as does the King James
Bible; the French Bible du semeur and the New English Bible give
"the man who must be lost." Here is Tyndale in 1534: "and none of
them is lost, but that lost child." One must have read all that Jesus
says in this prayer of his disciples, of these men he loved and for
whom he was responsible, to be struck, touched by the very simple
words "that lost child." I immediately felt Jesus's great sadness at
the perdition of Judas, whom he doubtless loved as much as the
other disciples and whom he considers in the Tyndale translation as
a child he has lost. (It is true that the word *child* at that time could
also mean a young man, but Tyndale guides the reader toward
the more usual sense of the word.) The translation is undoubtedly
wrong; the other translations quoted here give a better sense of the
expression. But Tyndale prompts one to reread in the Gospels the few
glimpses into the relationship between Jesus and Judas in order to
confirm or disprove this suggestion of a true tenderness in Jesus for
the one who was going to betray him.

6.

And what happens in the act of translating the Bible, of writing
in its place another prose, another poetry? I imagine an exemplary
translator who discovers that the process of translation is above all a
process of reading, more effective than ordinary reading, by which
he strains both to hear another voice and to hear it in his own lan-
guage. But this voice that resonates in the words that biblical writers
find by the usual work of writing is the voice of God; the world that
gradually takes shape is such as God sees it; the Other that one is
discovering is God in Person. Translating the Bible presents itself as
a spiritual exercise, the encounter with an absolute transcendence, a
commitment that requires much more than erudition and research.
I imagine that a well-informed Bible translator knows that he is
working out, here too, his salvation "with fear and trembling" (Phi-
lippians 2:12). (Again this salutary *fear* that one discovers at each
step in the New Testament.)

And Bible translation is not really comparable to translating
Virgil or Pushkin, for the Bible is unlike any other book. When
the disciples of Emmaus realize that the one who was speaking to
them was Jesus, they say to each other, "Did not our heart burn
within us . . . while he opened [*diènoigen*] to us the scriptures?"
(Luke 24:32). When they go back to the eleven disciples and their
companions in Jerusalem, Jesus appears once again, and Luke
notes that he "opened [*diènoixen*] their understanding, that they
might understand the scriptures" (Luke 24:45). We could think
that this does not concern us, since it was a matter of showing
Jewish followers the meaning of the Hebrew Bible that the arrival
of Jesus alone elucidated. However, when Lydia, a Macedonian,
was listening to evangelists preach, this same Luke writes that her
"heart the Lord opened [*diènoixe*] that she attended unto the things
which were spoken of Paul" (Acts 16:14). Neither can Christians

fathom the word of God without God's help. We too need him to open the Scriptures, to open our mind and our heart to, not just the superficial aspect of what is said, but to the depth of the voice that is speaking.

The Bible translator depends on the presence, beyond his own knowledge, of help from above. Translating the Bible in a spirit of humility would be a priceless act, the oft-repeated seeking and experience of that grace. And the biblical translator depends, as much as the poet and the translator of poetry, on a kind of inspiration. He too must receive, as if from nowhere, words, rhythms, sounds, syntactical forms. He too must learn what it is to write.

He must also know, as I have said, his own language. While reading recent translations of the Bible into English, I note, and I am not the only one, that this is rarely the case. Here are a few examples where one sees their platitude and lifelessness. First, the Jerusalem Bible: "Then Saul said to his armour-bearer, 'Draw your sword and run me through with it; I do not want these uncircumcised men to come and gloat over me.' But his armour-bearer was afraid and would not do it. So Saul took his own sword and fell on it" (1 Samuel 31:1–4).

The awkwardness of the English is remarkable—*with it, do it, on it*. The drama and the immense sadness of Israel's defeat and of her king's death, especially, disappear under an inert English.

Here is a sentence from the New English Bible: "Make no mistake about this: God is not to be fooled" (Galatians 6:7).

Whereas the Bible de Port-Royal grasps the conciseness of Paul's Greek and the urgency in his voice—"Do not be mistaken, one does not mock God" (and Tyndale's English, as well as the King James version, is even more powerful: "Be not deceived, God is not mocked")—Paul is transformed into a pedagogue who is a tiny bit verbose ("about this" is redundant), a little stiff or unnatural in his choice of words ("make no mistake"), and eager to keep a certain distance. The translators, not having heard the voice of the text, have missed its *meaning*.

The same observation regarding another letter distorted by the same translators: "Next a word to you who have great possessions. Weep and wail over the miserable fate descending on you" (James 5:1).

Not listening very well to their own language, they abruptly change registers between the first and second sentences. In the first, the same bureaucrat, perhaps sitting at his desk, informs the rich that he has something to say to them. In the second, he seems suddenly to imitate an Old Testament manner in order to speak of grave matters, but he completely misses the mark, "weep and wail" being a cliché, "miserable fate" belonging to Victorian English. Listen rather to the King James Version, which perfectly renders the pressing tone of the apostle, his prophet's voice: "Go to now, ye rich men, weep and howl for your miseries that shall come upon you."

Here, finally, is the most comical and most wretched passage, taken once again from the New English Bible: "Then he who sat on the throne said, 'Behold! I am making all things new!' And he said to me, 'Write this down; for these words are trustworthy and true. Indeed,' he said, 'they are already fulfilled'" (Revelation 21:5–6).

"Behold," which does belong to the elevated style, is nevertheless archaic; in "Write this down," on the other hand, we hear a boss speaking to his secretary. The last sentence completes the impression that God is addressing us with the formality of a gentleman, precise and conscientious.

These incompetent translations are not just errors in style, literary blunders. They prevent the Bible from speaking; they muffle the word of salvation; they hobble the work of the gospel. Recovering true Christianity requires *faithful* translations, faithful to the revelation such as it is expressed as well as to the never-exhausted resources of the translator's language, and full of an active, animating faith. The translation must be the deepening of the biblical faith and the language of the translator, who recognizes his ignorance little by little.

I have suggested that Bible translation is an art, and an art of hope. It is also an art of enjoyment and an art of loving. Whatever his frustrations, the translator must rejoice in handling his language, in the same way as the biblical writers themselves, always in search of terms, metaphors, cadences, and even wordplays that tell the truth and do not leave readers indifferent. One feels this pleasure, this tireless impatience, in the Jansenists of the Bible de Port-Royal, in Tyndale, in the King James translators. Why do we not sense it in a single modern English translation? What disaster has occurred to keep us from translating with strength?

In order to translate the Bible, one must love the God of the word and the word of God; wish the good of the Bible as one wishes the good of one's neighbor; love one's language and give its best; love the readers, write for God and for them. The Christian virtue associated with translation is faithfulness, but love seems even more essential to me. Translation is a charitable work. With it, transcendence becomes a real presence.

8

On Inspiration in Poetry

1.

In order to recover the true Christian faith and its works, we must, indeed, discern the inspiration of the biblical texts—a folly for non-Christians, a very often contested idea in our modern Christianity, tame and diluted as it is. The challenging untimeliness of Christianity also requires us to separate the inspiration of the Bible, the foundation of its authority and the cause of the alterity of its word, from "inspiration" in a great writer.

Let us recognize at the same time something that is obvious yet easily forgotten: we do not know what inspiration is. Faced with a poem by King David or by Paul Claudel, we cannot discern how the first was inspired, nor in what measure nor in what manner the second was. However, even our erroneous ways of speaking of inspiration are instructive. To exclaim about a given poem that the poet was inspired in writing it, whereas we know nothing of the sort (inspired by whom? by what?), shows clearly that we sense in the origin and composition of a well-written poem an element of mystery. To pretend that inspiration concerns only the seed of the poem and the flow of feelings, ideas, felicitous expressions of which the poet finds himself the vessel, while leaving to the intelligence the work of meticulously arranging the details of verses and the elaboration of form, seems an equally useful error. One refuses to see that the current passes thanks to the choice of a given word or a given comma, to the rejection of a given rhythm in favor of another, to numerous revisions, to continual erasures. That if inspiration exists, it operates also in the details, for the simple reason that the emotions, the sensations, the perspectives on reality are only present in the perfection of the completed work—*are not* prior to the verbal material that permits them to emerge. But in wishing to believe that the poem arrives by a kind of rapture, one concedes at least, once again, the mystery of poetry without seeing that this mystery pursues the poet in the advent of the least particularity of his poem.

One could moreover wonder in what way the inspiration of a poem can have any importance for readers, since it is the finished poem that touches them. In the case of a biblical poem, divine inspiration is capital, but above all as a fact and a presence, to be recognized by faith or rejected. Is the inspiration of nonbiblical poems spoken of because one likes to think that reading poetry puts us in contact with the strange, with *something else*?

As for the poet, he cannot know, as he reads his poems, whether they were inspired, nor, as he writes them, whether inspiration is guiding him. Does a series of lines come with a surprising facility? So much the better, but the brain, operating faster than consciousness, is perhaps at the origin of it, and those miraculous lines call often for severe modification or even erasure.

In order to advance, it is necessary to seek, regarding poems in the Bible—if we believe them inspired—what is possible to add to the fact that God wished them such as they are and that he was guiding their authors accordingly. As for extrabiblical poetry, we must listen, but with a critical spirit, to the very diverse witness of poets on the experience of the poetic act and probe our own experience, without having the assurance of interpreting it aright.

2.

As for the Christian poet, it seems dangerous for him to think himself inspired, giving the name *inspiration* to his own enthusiasm and the ease with which he conceives his poems and elicits the music of their language. Above all, he does not produce Scripture. He would love for God to watch over his poems, as with all his actions, and he does well to pray for this. But if there is reason to believe, objectively, that God inspires Christian poets as much in their work of composition as elsewhere, God alone knows it. It is better for the poet to accomplish his task without thinking of the inspiration that animates him, or does not animate him, while recalling this commandment from Jesus: "But when thou doest alms, let not thy left hand know what thy right hand doeth" (Matthew 6:3). This reference to the right hand encourages me to apply to the poet those famous words, and also that invitation to a kind of self-forgetfulness, which recalls humility (something one cannot attain knowingly) and eloquence, which concerns us more, and which comes when our attention is occupied by something else.

Other verses of the New Testament put us on our guard: "And the tongue is a fire, a world of iniquity: so is the tongue among our members, that it defileth the whole body, and setteth on fire the course of nature; and it is set on fire of hell" (James 3:6). The passage is frightening—such was certainly its intention!—if we grasp that, just as "a little fire" kindles "a great forest" (James 3:5, a better reading than that of the King James Version), so the tongue, inspired by Gehenna, is capable of effacing, in our eyes, the divine presence in the universe—as so many modern narratives have succeeded in doing. Whence the urgency of the prayer that Milton addresses to the Holy Spirit at the beginning of *Paradise Lost*: "What in me is dark / Illumine, what is low raise and support" (vv. 22–23). One must read the whole passage to grasp the depth of this supplication (and to hear the gathered-up strength of the verses), for Milton has just presented the spirit of God like this: "Thou from the first / Wast present, and with mighty wings outspread / Dove-like satst brooding on the vast Abyss / And mad'st it pregnant" (lines 19–22). As the Spirit brought forth creation out of the abyss, Milton prays to him to bring forth his epic from that which in him is equally base, and as God created light by separating it from darkness, he asks for his own darkness to be illumined.

Is this presumptuous? Perhaps, but Milton recognizes his indigence, his ignorance, his sin, and trusts himself to the great creative and luminous Power that is most capable of helping him. He finds himself in the position of Isaiah when the seraphim appear in the temple and sing the glory of God. "Woe is me!" he cries, "for I am undone; because I am a man of unclean lips, and I dwell in the midst of a people of unclean lips" (Isaiah 6:5). Before the vision of his epic-to-be, in which he aspires to "assert Eternal Providence, / And justify the ways of God to men" (vv. 25–26), Milton also takes cognizance of the darkness that inhabits him. Does he also think of another of Jesus's sayings—"That which cometh out of the mouth, this defileth a man" (Matthew 15:11)?

Milton's prayer is legitimate—even if we are totally incapable of deciding whether or not it was heard: to speak of the inspiration of *Paradise Lost* is simply to translate our astonishment before the quality of such an imagination and of such writing. To ask for inspiration to illumine one's darkness recognizes that all poets, no matter how Christian, have "unclean lips," and happily distances us from a certain reflection on inspiration, that of Henri Bremond and Jacques Maritain in particular, which assumed that divine inspiration descended into the being of the Christian poet to find there a just and good deeper self.

Continuing to reflect on the sources of the poem, Milton leaves divine inspiration to explore a real dependence, equally mysterious and more interesting because it is analyzable. He turns, at the beginning of book 7 of his epic, no longer to the Holy Spirit but to Urania, the muse of celestial poetry. He imagines that it is she, in particular her "voice" (line 2), who has guided him so far; that it is she who has protected him during his "presumptuous" voyage into "the Heaven of Heavens" (line 13) and who has in some way furnished him his poem, visiting him by night as he slept (lines 28–29). But what, for Milton and for us, does the intervention of "Urania," this muse invented by poets, mean? Milton seems to sense, in writing, a force, an intelligence that one had better not confuse with the Holy Spirit, an enigmatic presence on whom, above all, he *depends*. On the point of finally telling the story of the fall in book 9, conscious of the fact of being himself fallen in a fallen world and not able to say as it should be said the very moment that separated us both from God and from speech at the same time good, beautiful, true, and natural—the speech of Adam and Eve before the fall—he evokes once again Urania without naming her and in the third person. He will successfully complete his project, he writes, "If answerable style I can obtain / Of my celestial patroness, who deigns / Her nightly visitation unimplored, / And dictates to me slumbering; or inspires / Easy my unpremeditated verse" (lines 20–24).

Why at night? Why this feeling of writing a poem that is dictated to him? Of finding verses without having thought them? Above all, can one believe him? It seems to me that one can, for he describes in his own way, with an imagination and a perception of the poetic act that are beyond the reach of ordinary poets, a universal experience.

Poetry is always given. The poet works like Adam after he had eaten the forbidden fruit: "by the sweat of [their] brow," he does not arrive at his ends, he starts over, he suffers the frustration of defeat, and if ideas, images, emotions, sonorities come, and please him, they *come*, indeed, but from where? From the unconscious? From the subconscious? From the buried and generally inaccessible memory? From elsewhere? The poetic act is always, seen from this perspective, nocturnal; it leads you, like the moon, to the other side of the world and the other side of the self. One truly has the sense of being *visited*. To speak of dictation is a felicitously exaggerated way of translating the astonishment of the poet at what he manages to conceive, at the rightness and the music of verses that sometimes seem, after multiple unfruitful attempts, to write themselves.

Whence the marveling tone with which he speaks of his "celestial patroness," and whence the reality of this feminine presence. If masculine poets invented the Muses, it is no doubt because they knew obscurely that their poetry was the work of the feminine part of their being, or rather of something in them that seemed *other*. Poetry really is other, and Milton—the most masculine, willful, independent, combative of poets—must have felt very deeply this gentle presence. A few verses later, fearing that the unpropitious era or his advanced age might prevent him from finishing his poem, he sees that that certainly will be the case "if all be mine, / Not hers, who brings it nightly to my ear" (lines 46–47).

Milton first prays for the Holy Spirit to help him, before recognizing that he is rather dealing with Urania, a fiction whom he addresses thus: "heavenly-born, / Before the hills appeared, or fountain flowed, / Thou with eternal Wisdom didst converse, / Wisdom thy sister, and with her didst play / In presence of the Almighty Father, pleased / With thy celestial song" (book 7, lines 7–12). "Urania" is the name of the song that emanates from God, that harmonized the whole of creation, that animates the song of creation, even fallen ("The pastures . . . the valleys . . . shout for joy, they also sing," Psalm 65:13), and that links our purely human poetry to the celestial songs. Poetry presents itself not as a special means for men to express themselves but as the sonorous image of the song that is found in the heart of the All. In an entirely realistic perspective, Urania stands for the surprise, the alterity of poetic creation, the poem as gift.

3.

Wordsworth substitutes an earthly wind for the Holy Spirit and goes further than Milton in exploring the inability to write. At the beginning of *The Prelude*, he recounts his return to the Lake District and his aspiration to write poem after poem. Here are his first words:

> O there is blessing in this gentle breeze,
> A visitant that while it fans my cheek
> Doth seem half-conscious of the joy it brings
> From the green fields, and from yon azure sky.

The breath of poetic inspiration is perceived in a wind in the north of England, which, a natural presence, caresses the poet's cheek. The breeze nevertheless brings a blessing, and as a "visitant" it becomes a supernatural presence. It "come[s]," according to the next verse, with a "mission." Unlike Milton (blind and sedentary), Wordsworth discovers, in walking, that he feels inspired when he is conscious of his body and his surroundings—that a quasi-supernatural inspiration makes itself felt in the wind that greets him. He receives a kind of inspiration from reality by opening himself to a force in nature that transcends nature. His point of view is not Christian, but his intuition of a material world that is more than material and that lives its own life, immense and exhilarating, recaptures, among others, the vision of the Psalms.

However, inspiration turns in on itself, and this only a few verses further on:

> For I, methought, while the sweet breath of heaven
> Was blowing on my body, felt within
> A correspondent breeze, that gently moved
> With quickening virtue, but is now become
> A tempest, a redundant energy,
> Vexing its own creation.
>
> (ll. 33–38)

Once again the breath of heaven blows on his body, the hesitation between the natural and the supernatural expressing itself here in the ambiguity of the word "heaven," but the similar breeze that he discovers in himself develops an energy, not "exuberant" but "redundant," and little by little is destroyed. He realizes he cannot write. The experience repeats itself and seems definitive:

> It was a splendid evening, and my soul
> Once more made trial of her strength, nor lacked
> Æolian visitations; but the harp
> Was soon defrauded, and the banded host
> Of harmony dispersed in straggling sounds,
> And lastly utter silence!
>
> (ll. 94–99)

"And lastly utter silence!"—at the beginning of a very long poem, these words stun the reader, as the experience that they recreate must have shaken Wordsworth.

Wordsworth finds, of course, a way out of the silence, very original and still more surprising. After having wondered if the circumstances of his childhood and his youth, which seemed to be preparing him for a life of poetry, had been in vain, he continues to speak of his childhood, recounting it in detail without going back to those moments of defeat, and the reader understands then that the poem Wordsworth was to write is precisely the one he is in the process of composing. Beautiful allegory, tacit, never made explicit, for inspiration: it leads you elsewhere, it comes in writing.

4.

With Milton we observe a Christian poet who hopes to receive a supernatural—divine—inspiration, while wary of his audacity and seeking to put himself in harmony with the continuous song of creation he calls Urania. Wordsworth, without believing himself inspired by God, sees nonetheless, in the breath that comes to him from the natural world, a mysterious blessing. In order to understand that possible superhuman dimension of inspiration, must one not explore also the perfectly natural and explainable ways by which the poet receives his poetry? And begin with language? Language speaks to the poet; if he is a poet, it is partly for that reason. He listens to his language, he hears, in the first place, less the, say, logical links created by grammar and syntax than the sounds of words and the movement of sentences. He is inspired by language, which moves him to write. As Claudel says in his "Letter to Abbé Bremond on Poetic Inspiration," the poet "has been launched . . . by a kind of rhythmic excitement, of repetition and verbal swaying, of measured recitation"—in the manner, I would say, of a musician: whatever might be the emotions or thoughts that he seeks to make appear, he is immersed more than anything in the *matter* of his art. Language carries the poet as the universe of sounds carries the musician. He also understands that the most mysterious virtue of language is to transform everything it touches, adding, for example, to the most "objective" description of a landscape, a human presence, sounds, cadences, a syntax. A poem, in which the slightest syllable names and sings, becomes almost the object he marries, and the object becomes, in our minds, the poem: it changes under the influence of a poetic light.

Language "inspires" the poet; reality as well. Absolutely any apparently insignificant parcel of that strange All that sustains us can call him, capture his attention, launch him into the course of questions, or rather repetitions of a single question, whose gravity children understand but adults little by little lose the habit of asking: "Why?" Claudel is right to declare, in "Religion and Poetry," that a poet "loves to take seriously all the things that surround him": if he is a Christian, because anything can be the object of praise, and, in any event, because the next poem can come from anywhere. The poet thus drawn knows in some degree an experience that Wordsworth describes marvelously in "Tintern Abbey." There exists, he says, a "blessed mood" in which, "the breath of this corporeal frame / And even the motion of our human blood / Almost suspended," we become "a living soul" and "we see into the life of things." It is the inspiration upstream of the poem, which is assuredly not given to us all with the same depth but can surprise, I believe, at any moment and not just poets: at the sight, for example, of the trees' silence and immobility on a June night, in a garden where the pale light reveals the strange and other life of the natural world. And intuitions, sometimes dazzling perceptions also emerge in the act of writing, as if "the things that surround us" wished to communicate to us their manner of being, move us to put them into poetry.

Certain Shakespeare comedies—such as *A Midsummer Night's Dream*, *The Merchant of Venice*, and *As You Like It*—in which one passes from one place to another and sometimes to a third still more numinous, fascinate us, I think, in part because they represent these moments of inspiration, during which the mind travels both farther and farther and closer and closer to the heart of things, toward the extreme of elsewhere and here.

Claudel speaks of this initiative of the world to approach the poet in "The Muses," the first of his *Five Grand Odes*. He first addresses the "poet's Muse" in these terms: "You contemplate each thing in your heart, for each thing you seek *how to say it!*"—the poet's task, indeed, being not to describe the world, nor even, essentially, to write it, but to say it, to make it appear afresh in the sounds, the music, the song of poetry. And he continues: "I have found the secret; I know how to speak; if I wish, I can tell you / that which each thing *wishes to say.*" Here is a joyous wordplay that allows him to suggest that things *wish to say*[1] what they *mean*, that they insist on expressing themselves through the mouthpiece of the poet.

Inspiration through reality assumes that, before being a man who writes poems, the poet lives poetically, ceaselessly attentive to a world become poetry in his gaze and ready to make him speak. A third source of inspiration is everything that is hidden within the poet. His memory in the first place, a creative power that transforms the past through the present gaze and the present through the past's return. The brain also inspires, thanks to its unseen work, its incessant placing into relationship innumerable data from our sensations, emotions, ideas, encounters. It works faster than we and often independently of consciousness, most obviously during sleep. It furnishes unexpected images, surprising perceptions, sudden cadences, emotions foreign to those we were experiencing. Then the unconscious's contribution is such that, if we delve into a certain experience in order to discover and define it in its fullness, there enter so many other ingredients that the experience offered by the poem is different, new and unforeseen. In a sense, all poems are impersonal: the

---

1   In French, the expression for the verb "to mean" is an idiom, whose literal meaning is "to wish to say."

poet who is most determined to "express himself," to say precisely what he feels, to *conceive well* in order to *state clearly* (Boileau), finds himself ultimately before a poem studded with surprises. One does not choose words; words choose you.

It is certain that the poet, in the act of writing, is inhabited by something, whence the very ancient idea of the poet as a *vates*, a seer inspired by a Muse. But this something is most often everything that, within him and in his relationship with reality, escapes his consciousness. A last inspiration is the poem in the process of writing itself. It too gives ideas; words suddenly associate to reveal relationships among phenomena that one had not seen, rhythms launch themselves, a music makes itself heard. At the sound of the words, one sees doors opening. The poem speaks to you, unfinished and full of desires. Before its revision—and even in this period where the poet is conscious especially of reflecting, critiquing, proposing exact and minute changes—it is the poem somehow that leads the way. Any poem is an advent, and Claudel felicitously quotes, in "Poetry Is an Art," these words from Ecclesiasticus 32:3 in the Apocrypha: "Hinder not musick." As God places his words in Jeremiah's mouth (Jeremiah 1:9) and causes Ezekiel to eat a scroll (Ezekiel 2:8–3:3), so, at a very ordinary level but no less strange, the poet discovers in himself a poem that is seeking to see the light of day. A poem that seems to have a will of its own and an autonomous life.

5.

Which leads me to biblical poetry and to inspiration properly speaking: to works, according to Paul in his second letter to Timothy, "given by inspiration of God" (2 Timothy 3:16). In studying that inspiration, one is often surprised. The prophets sometimes recognize that they are incapable of speaking, or of speaking well. As soon as the Lord announces to Jeremiah that he has established him a prophet to the nations, Jeremiah cries out, "Ah, . . . I cannot speak" (Jeremiah 1:6). I have already quoted Isaiah as saying, before the vision of God at the moment of his calling, "Woe is me! for I am undone; / because I am a man of unclean lips" (Isaiah 6:5). At least one of the psalmists feels within himself, on the contrary, the poem ready to come forth:

> My heart is inditing a good matter:
> I speak of the things which I have made touching the king:
> my tongue is the pen of a ready writer.
>
> (Psalm 45:1)

Another, at the end of an impassioned poem on the wonders of creation and of the Law, in a moment of self-examination hopes that all he says and thinks will be acceptable:

> Let the words of my mouth,
> and the meditation of my heart,
> be acceptable in thy sight, O Lord,
> my strength, and my redeemer.
>
> (Psalm 19:14)

It is touching to think that a poet, certainly inspired, feels the need to assure himself before God that his work, in its conception and its writing, is not faulty.

One understands why in rereading the psalm, which begins with these famous verses:

> The heavens declare the glory of God;
> and the firmament sheweth his handywork.
> Day unto day uttereth speech,
> and night unto night sheweth knowledge.

The universe, created by God, by the Word, is already naturally inspired, so to speak. In Psalm 98, the mountains are invited to "be joyful together" (Psalm 98:8), and the whole universe, from one end to the other of Psalm 148, to "praise the Lord." But in the most fervent poem, the reader feels the weight of sin. Who knows what unwilled evil slips into the most seriously and prudently considered poem? A biblical writer too can fear not having been up to the task (even if afterward we assume he was), for it is clear that God uses, for the Scriptures, perfectly human beings with their character, their aptitudes, the circumstances of their life and particular ways of inhabiting the world. Accepting the most elevated doctrine of inspiration of the Bible does not preclude us from believing, as I said in *Bible et poésie*, that these inspired poets hesitated, sought fruitlessly, took a different path, were stressed over not being able to move forward, rejected a given image or syntactical form, erased what did not please them, before ending up, like any other poet, with a finally satisfying work, over which they must have rejoiced. Their doubts and their pleasures make completely real the human dimension of divine words. Whether it be a psalmist or the author of Job, of Proverbs, of the Song of Songs, of Lamentations.

Lamentations, along with Psalm 119, surprises us more than any other biblical poem when we read it in light of inspiration or simply of poetry. These five poems, probably composed in Palestine after the ruin of Jerusalem in 587 and the work of a single author who may not have been Jeremiah, are famous for the poetic excellence of their complaints, the depth of their emotion. Yet the first four are acrostic poems: they each consist of 22 verses, the first verse beginning with the first letter of the Hebrew alphabet, the second with the second letter, and so on. The third poem follows this rule even more rigorously, since the three lines of each verse begin with the corresponding letter. The fifth abandons the alphabet but hints at it by its 22 verses. "Strange way to conceive poetry!" one would say before such an artifice, bothersome for the poet and apparently arbitrary. Other constraints, those of prosody, do not hinder the arrival of poetry; quite the contrary, they help the poet seek what *is to be said* and discover it by inventing it. But what relationship could exist among the complaint, the anger, the guilt, the despair, and the necessity of successively declining, by the choice of the first words of the verses, the letters of the alphabet? And how to reconcile inspiration with a schema that appears arid at first glance?

Or should one see in this strange rigor a great lesson on inspiration? If it is not to be excluded that biblical inspiration arrives through a sort of ecstasy, it comes most often through the normal labor of the poet, and it makes the modalities of Hebrew poetry his own. Here it goes further: it imposes on the poet a singular discipline, it compels him to satisfy the requirements of the acrostic form, it accompanies him in the search for words whose first letter fits into a predetermined structure, and it appears just as much in these details as in the agonizing complaint that rises from the poems.

For, well considered, this wise foolishness of acrostic poems is founded on something solid. Following the Hebrew alphabet, after all, has nothing gratuitous about it: a poem thus constituted achieves a formal completeness, places itself under the aegis of the language in which it is written, and respects, by sounding out its letters, one after another, the language that God chooses to speak to men. I sense that a rapport exists between such a submission to the language and the great themes of Lamentations.

Does not this patient attention to a simple aspect of the poems' form participate in the search for poetic pleasure? People speak, at least since Aristotle, of the pleasure of poetry; Claudel scatters throughout his essays a more stimulating word: *delectation.* Whatever the subject of a poem, the poet always seeks to delight himself and, in the very material of his writings, to make the reader share his pleasure. Lamentations—which concerns the destruction of Jerusalem, the inhabitants' suffering, God's anger, and his separation from his people—presents itself as a work quite foreign to pleasure, in which the poet's and the reader's delectation could seem inappropriate and contradictory. Yet what does God inspire in the poet? How does he guide him to speak of the devastation he is contemplating?

The first poem concentrates all the suffering of defeat and of its consequences in figures of speech. It is first the city of Jerusalem that is suffering:

> She weepeth sore in the night,
> and her tears are on her cheeks.
> Among all her lovers
> she hath none to comfort her.
> All her friends have dealt treacherously with her,
> they are become her enemies!
>
> (Lamentations 1:2)

Then the Kingdom of Judah, personified as a woman:

> Judah is gone into captivity because of affliction,
> and because of great servitude.
> She dwelleth among the heathen,
> she findeth no rest.
> All her persecutors overtook her
> between the straits.
>
> (Lamentations 1:3)

Then Zion, another name for Jerusalem:

> The ways of Zion do mourn,
> because none come to the solemn feasts.

All her gates are desolate,
her priests sigh,
her virgins are afflicted,
and she is in bitterness!

(Lamentations 1:4)

Jerusalem "weepeth sore in the night"; Zion "is in bitterness": through these personifications, the inhabitants' affliction becomes, in a certain way, *fictional.* Without losing any of its reality, on the contrary, this affliction leads the reader into the country of poetry; it interests him and rejoices him at the same time that it touches him. For the effect to be complete, the poet transforms Judah, ordinarily masculine, into a feminine being, in the manner of Jerusalem and of Zion. This composite figure becomes, in the second half of the poem, a grand and dolorous feminine voice (personification evolves into prosopopoeia), the lamentation not being that of the poet, nor of any individual, but that of a city, of a country, of a mountain.

Another delectation for the poet and the reader: the metaphor, which comes into play as soon as the first words: "How doth the city sit solitary, that was full of people!" The complaint of the last eleven verses, among, let us say, realistic glimpses—"My virgins and my young men / are gone into captivity" (Lamentations 1:18); "My priests and mine elders / gave up the ghost in the city" (Lamentations 1:19)—multiplies the metaphorical representations of the punitive actions applied by the Lord:

From above hath he sent fire
into my bones, and it prevaileth against them.
He hath spread a net for my feet,
he hath turned me back.

. . .

The yoke of my transgressions is bound by his hand:
they are wreathed and come up upon my neck.

. . .

The Lord hath trodden the virgin, the daughter of Judah,
    as in a winepress.

(Lamentations 1:13–15)

It is not sufficient to speak of the figurative exuberance of
Hebrew poetry, nor to suppose that metaphor, like all other rhe-
torical figures, intervenes only to amplify the passion, embellish
the discourse, vary the style. These metaphors, also *fictions* them-
selves, transpose the people's despondency into a poetic vision that
is attractive and pleasing by transforming the real, making living
images file before us, bringing together dissimilar things.

The simile comes from the same source—the poetic imagination
at work even when the emotions to be explored are terrible—and
it produces a similar effect. The second poem, a cry of horror at
Jerusalem's distress and especially at a God of wrath who ceaselessly
destroys, throws off simile after simile. Upon the daughter of Zion's
tabernacle, the Lord "poured out his fury like fire" (Lamentations
2:4); the enemy's roar in the house of the Lord resounds "as in
the day of a solemn feast!" (Lamentations 2:7); in the streets of the
city, the hungry children "swooned as the wounded" (Lamentations
2:12). Let the daughter of Zion react: "pour out thine heart like
water / before the face of the Lord" (Lamentations 2:19). Each time,
an image appears that takes us out of reality, as well as rendering
it more present, and speaks to us of poetry, of its pleasure in trans-
figuring an event, an emotion, a seen object, by putting it suddenly
in relationship with a quite *other* phenomenon. Hence the force of
verse 13: "What thing shall I liken to thee, O daughter of Jerusa-
lem?" This purely rhetorical question—Jerusalem's suffering being
literally incomparable—takes on a singular meaning in a poet who

is ceaselessly comparing. Jerusalem seems to evade poetry, but the poet recovers poetry immediately by a voluntarily extravagant simile: "Thy breach is great like the sea."

But why the delectation in such a poem? If we believe Lamentations to be inspired, why did God spur its poet to seek, for himself and for the reader, a pleasure so foreign to its subject? Judah's situation is perhaps hopeless: despite the recognition of the people's sins, their prayers, and the poet's conviction that "Thou, O Lord, remainest forever" (Lamentations 5:19), the very last words cry out, trembling, for his help:

> Renew our days as of old.
> But thou hast utterly rejected us;
> thou art very wroth against us.
>
> (Lamentations 5:21–22)

The poet even seems to accuse God. He knows well that God has acted with justice because Judah has rebelled against him. However, the violence of God seems ferocious to him in the second poem and, one might say, inhumane: "The Lord hath swallowed up all the habitations of Jacob, and hath not pitied" (Lamentations 2:2), "he hath thrown down, / and hath not pitied" (Lamentations 2:17), "thou hast slain them in the day of thine anger / thou hast killed, and not pitied" (Lamentations 2:21). And here is how Jerusalem addresses him:

> Behold, O Lord, and
> consider to whom thou hast done this.
> Shall the women eat their fruit
> and children of a span long?
> Shall the priest and the prophet be slain in the sanctuary
>   of the Lord?
>
> (Lamentations 2:20)

The city asks God, in short, to realize what he has done and to judge whether it was truly necessary to go so far in his vengeance. In the last words—"Those that I have swaddled and brought up / hath mine enemy consumed"—one no longer can tell who is the enemy, the Babylonians or God. The poet sees further in the third poem, recognizing that God does not reject men forever, that if he afflicts them, "yet will he have compassion / according to the multitude of his mercies" (Lamentations 3:32), and that, both evil and good proceeding from "the mouth of the most High," man, instead of murmuring, would do better to accept "the punishment of his sins" (Lamentations 3:38–39). But this accent of revolt, with the sentiment that there is no apparent possibility of escape from the situation, could render all delectation vain and out of place.

Yet in reading the poem we realize, without the help of any theory of poetic pleasure, that we are taking pleasure in it, that the imagination is leading us into a reality that is changing before our eyes, continually enriching itself: into a world where the princes of Judah "are become like harts / that find no pasture" (Lamentations 1:6), where God becomes "as a bear lying in wait, / and as a lion in secret places" (Lamentations 3:10). Leaving aside the prosody, the verses, the rhythm, the sound, since we almost all read translations. Even in translation, one senses something other than pain and affliction in a verse like this one:

> Is it nothing to you, all ye that pass by?
> Behold, and see if there be any sorrow like
> unto my sorrow, which is done unto me,
> wherewith the Lord hath afflicted me
> in the day of his fierce anger.
>
> (Lamentations 1:12)

It is true that we read these poems at our leisure: they speak of a disaster befallen long ago, and we know the rest of the story. The poet and his first readers or listeners were living in the middle of the drama. Yes, but must not their delighting in the poems have brought precisely the hope the Jews needed? The poetry was taking on the disaster and rising above it by offering, in the middle of the desolation, its opposite, the creativity of man and the unsearchable treasury of language. The poetry of Lamentations transcends lamentation. And it is *this* that God inspires. The gift of the poem reveals, not his wrath, but his goodness.

Should we not be astonished, incidentally, that he also inspires criticism of himself? If the second poem is "inspired by God" (to return to Paul's assertion), one must believe that he has suggested, or at least tolerated and accepted in his word, those complaints in the second poem that call him to witness to his own cruelty. It seems that God, knowing from the inside all that we suffer, blesses, at least temporarily, even our panic and our revolt.

The delectation—I would say the joy—of biblical poetry speaks to the reader of the joy that transcends lamentation, as it transcends the alarming things the prophets often declare. We are dealing, after all, with language, which enjoys a relationship—one we cannot grasp—with the word of God, by which he created the universe. The language of purely human poetry, or the one we prosaically utter every day, is already a gift: an allusion, an indication. That of biblical poetry, inspired by God, is a way to God and a sign, perhaps, of his own joy. We do not understand inspiration, but we do understand that God inspires at the same time what the poems say, and the prose texts, and their ways of saying it. That he is just as concerned with their art as with the truths they convey. And it is, it seems to me, in that art, apparently superfluous and irrelevant to the "message," that the message culminates.

9

Seek and Ye Shall Find

1.

The "good news," joy, inspiration can seem quite far away, and I repeat what I was saying at the beginning of this book. God does not ask us to believe in his existence as we believe in that of Mongolia, nor to approve of Christianity as we might approve, for example, of the republican form of government. He invites us to *know* him, by the mediation of Christ. However, the faith that would give us this knowledge is located beyond our reach. A gift of God, it depends on him; it comes from elsewhere. We cannot produce it ourselves. It constitutes another means of knowing than those we already possess and is necessary for us to see another dimension in the real; it constitutes almost another organ, which we need in order to live fully.

Here indeed is the Bible's teaching. But what then to say to whoever would like to have faith but cannot manage to reach it?

That there is nothing to be done? That faith will come or will not come? That he must prepare himself to be definitively disappointed, excluded from grace?

Listen instead to what Jesus tells him:

Ask, and it shall be given you;
Seek, and ye shall find;
Knock, and it shall be opened unto you:
For every one that asketh receiveth;
And he that seeketh findeth;
And to him that knocketh it shall be opened.
                              (Matthew 7:7–8; Luke 11:9–10)

Jesus thus composes, apparently speaking spontaneously, a brief poem according to the norms of Hebrew poetry. Each verse, while saying essentially the same thing three times from slightly different perspectives, follows the rule of synonymic parallelism, in the manner of the Old Testament poets, such as Isaiah:

Seek ye the Lord while he may be found,
Call ye upon him while he is near.
                                        (Isaiah 55:6)

In so doing, he emphasizes the necessity of seeking and the certainty of finding, by reiterating and then again reiterating the same promise. And is not the very expression of these invitations astonishing? Does it not take our breath away? Jesus does not say that if one seeks, one will perhaps find, nor that one will have a good chance of finding, nor even that it is very probable that one will find. He says, with all the authority of the Son of God, "Seek and *ye shall find*. . . . He that seeketh *findeth*." The promise is marvelous, invigorating, divine.

Truth be told, each time I concentrate on a passage of the Bible, I discover how much the revelation is made to astonish us.

The same overture and the same assurance are found in other calls, which, coming from Jesus, are also commands. He cries out before the crowd that has come to Jerusalem for a religious feast, "If any man thirst, let him come unto me, and drink" (John 7:37). *Seek and ye shall find; come, ye thirsty, and drink.* And this thirst is not defined, as in the Beatitudes, where it is those who hunger and thirst "after righteousness" who will be filled (Matthew 5:6).

Here whoever is seeking is not asked to thirst for justice—nor for purity, nor pardon—but simply to thirst and to approach Jesus, compelled by a vital need. Jesus cries out at another moment, "Come unto me, all ye that labor and are heavy laden, and I will give you rest" (Matthew 11:28). "I will give you rest": it is enough to *come*. Jesus's poem seems to be addressed to everyone. It is true that in the Gospel of Luke, Jesus, after having taught the Lord's Prayer to the disciples, continues (perhaps at another moment), saying that, if men finally do give to those who ask, the Father gives liberally, and therefore "ask and it shall be given you" (Luke 11:9). The invitation to seek and find concerns, not unbelievers, but disciples and, as in the Lord's Prayer, all Christians. However, in the Gospel of Matthew, the distinction between the disciples and the listeners in general remains intentionally uncertain. In the series of discourses that cover chapters 5 through 7, Jesus addresses sometimes the disciples, sometimes the crowds, sometimes both. At the end of all these discourses, Matthew reports that the teaching of Jesus, who spoke with authority whereas the scribes relied on tradition, astonished "the people" (Matthew 7:28). It is quite naturally to the crowds that the words "seek and ye shall find" are addressed—those who, though they did not know God, were not indifferent to him.

Concerning the disciples also, and now Christians, the proposition changes slightly in meaning. Their lives become, ideally, the uninterrupted quest for what they have already found, an asking, a seeking, a desire to enter constantly repeated and constantly granted.

As in so many passages of the Gospels, these chapters of Matthew blend words destined for distinct categories of people and resonate far beyond the moment in history and the particular circumstances. Jesus's transcendence in relation to linear time permits him to address each generation and the entire world, the Christian and the seeker. To speak intimately to each. The promise is always, for everyone, that he who seeks shall find.

2.

Indeed, on the occasions when the way of salvation is presented, in the Gospels and in the Acts of the Apostles, no one warns the listeners that the required faith depends on God and remains unattainable by their own efforts. Jesus invites them to *seek*, to *come*; Peter and Paul unveil the facts of the "good news," centered on the death and resurrection of Jesus, in order for them to accept and act accordingly. Paul explains to the Athenians, who have no knowledge of the story of salvation, that God's will was for men everywhere to "seek" the Lord in order, if possible, to "find him" (Acts 17:27). He who seeks need not preoccupy himself with the doctrine of faith and grace.

Unfortunately, there are numerous aberrant ways of seeking, by following paths that do not permit us to find. We have been thus constituted since the fall: we go off in all directions, pursue mirages, complicate what is simple, and labor to achieve focus. It will be useful, before exploring the gospel way of seeking, to reflect on the other ways, to lay out a kind of anatomy of erroneous seeking—not for the intellectual pleasure of understanding and categorizing, but, if possible, to help the seeker avoid going astray.

Let us begin with the thirst for the absolute. It corresponds to a correct intuition and seeks rightly to satisfy (to quote the *Journal* of

Maine de Biran) "the need . . . to attach oneself to something . . . changeless," which would save us from the flux present within us and in the world. It assumes, or wishes, ardently and anxiously, to be able to assume that at the very heart of reality there exists a transcendence, whatever its nature; perhaps a stable permanence foreign to the shifting shadows among which we flounder, an imperative of life ordained by the real, a state of consciousness beyond what we ordinarily experience. But how easy it is to slip into the illusion of a transfigured self, attained through drugs, sex, or violence, to have the conviction of being called to kill for a good cause, to believe in "the absolute Being!"—an intransitive expression, so to speak, that refers to nothing and projects us toward an august nothingness. Or in the chimera of a cosmic energy, of spiritual intermediaries, and who knows what else?

Then the quest of the sovereign good, which can seem a little antiquated in our day but also possesses a certain virtue. To pursue the sovereign good as the one thing to prefer above all else is to act as in the parable where Jesus compares the Kingdom of Heaven to a merchant who, having found a pearl of great price, sells everything he owns to buy it (Matthew 13:45–46). It is to recognize that there exists a supreme goal to be attained and to accept, on condition of thinking like Aristotle, that the important thing is the orientation, not of the intelligence alone, but of the entirety of one's life. However, not everyone sees it this way, and opinions regarding the sovereign good are as varied as the faces in a crowd. (Montaigne and Pascal were greatly distressed over this.) It is often identified as happiness, which represents, for the serious seeker, a trap. Jesus does not promise to make us happy. He offers eminently desirable things: sight to the blind, healing to lepers, a door that opens to all who knock, but not happiness, such as we might conceive it. He offers instead, as to the Samaritan woman at Jacob's well, "a well of water springing up into everlasting life" (John 4:14), the joy of paradise experienced, at our level and despite our fallen nature, beginning now.

One must not seek the sovereign good in the known—in pleasures, honors, study, contemplation—but in the unknown, in what lies beyond our conception of reality. Must one then call God the sovereign good? That undoubtedly resembles a quest for the otherworldly, and God is assuredly our incomparable and supreme good—but what a dangerous ploy! God does not present himself that way, not being the God of the deists, and by thus conceiving him, we would follow our own ways of thinking rather than biblical revelation.

Then there is the idea of the sacred, which seems to respond perfectly to this desire for *something else*. If one is seeking, would it not be profitable to discern and venerate, wherever we find them, the signs of its presence? But the *sacred*, as I said in the second chapter, is again a snare. The intuition of another dimension, numinous, divine in the real, can very well open the mind's eyes and encourage a true quest, but to pursue the sacred in itself diverts us from the only way that arrives. One can be religiously moved at the Egyptians' notion of the sacred: What could be more imposing, more unbounded in relation to our smallness, than the representations of their gods? Or at the Greeks' sacred: What could be more inspiring than the intelligence of light and number in their temples? Or even at the rituals and sacrifices of the Aztecs, which contradict, by their radical foreignness, the normality in which we imprison ourselves? And so on, from one region, continent, and culture to the other. However, by marveling from a distance at such presences of the sacred, to appreciate and compare them, one becomes a simple connoisseur of spiritualities. A first step toward Christian reality would be to recognize that the ancient civilizations, including those that can appear rudimentary, opened themselves broadly to what transcended them and to wonder what kind of religious experience is to be discovered in our reduced and reductive modernity.

The *pietas* of the Romans offers an attractive version of the sacred when it proposes that all earthly places are sacred because of the deities that inhabit them. The material world would be in a sense divine and not limited to the descriptions of it provided by the whole of our science. This sense of place, of the mysterious character of any landscape, is found again in the sentiment of nature as a numinous presence, a sentiment that reigned for a long time in Europe as a religion of substitution, capable of creating all sorts of emotional and aesthetic satisfactions and liberated, if one so desired, from any obligation regarding God. The conviction that matter has its own life, thanks to its relationship with the divine, is legitimate (creation lives, for Christians, by the power of its creator and rejoices in his presence) and can lead very far. Even the most banal sentiment of a possible sacred in the visible universe—that caused by the sight of the night sky—can open the way, especially if one wonders why the wonderment before the stars and their incommensurable abode is so widespread and if one seeks to know the why of this extravagant superfluity of bodies and space. However, by interesting oneself in Christianity within the perspective of the sacred, one reduces it: one seeks the sacred in churches, in priests and their sacerdotal vestments, in rituals seen from the outside and admired for themselves, without the meaning of the buildings and ceremonies coming into play. For the problem of the sacred is that it encourages one to stop short of God, as in the quest of the pure, the entirely other, the transcendental. By seeking the sacred, rather than the Creator and Savior God who is its source and reason for being, one is once again taking the wrong path.

Next comes the search for a religion. "Ah, if only I had your faith!" often means that one would like to be in the warmth of a comforting belief, which would enable one to envisage the future and each day in serenity of mind, no longer to ask questions without answers. To benefit from what is termed highly inadequately "the consolation of faith." One may desire faith in order to settle the religious problem, without a real God bothering us by intervening in our plans. Having faith would amount, in short, to living one's life without needing to be occupied with God. The search for a religion can also be motivated by the need to let oneself be guided, by the aspiration to gain admittance to a protective structure, to venerable rituals, soothing and complex, to surround oneself with people having the same ideas, the same tastes. One can feel a certain satisfaction in being Catholic in France, Anglican in England, Lutheran in Norway, in embracing a certain way of organizing the "spiritual" consecrated by time, in belonging to a community that transcends borders.

One can also turn toward religion for the reason that atheists give in the first place, so as to explain belief in the supernatural: through the fear of life and the dread of death, to protect oneself from the threats of the world and to be able to envisage surviving extinction. From the Christian point of view, this reaction to the human condition is not entirely without foundation. By the fear of reality one recognizes at least that the natural world is diseased, one glimpses the fallen state of the world of men, and this fear does not appear exaggerated when one knows that Jesus calls Satan "the prince of this world" (John 12:31, 14:30, 16:11). The desire for immortality is related to a rightful intuition: we were not created to die; a new birth and an eternal life are offered to us. As for the most common and least demanding form of wonderment, that which leaves us speechless at the unimaginable profusion of stars, the most primitive emotions—which sometimes engender, it is true, perfectly vain superstitions—are nevertheless closer to the truth than a considered, reasonable, and unbelieving attitude. Closer, but at the same time, if they do not end in the discovery of God, quite far away.

One could also seek to establish the superiority of Christianity before committing oneself to it. What could be more sensible on the face of it? When faced with the proliferation of religions, why choose one, without having examined at least a few others? Becoming a Christian because one lives in a Christian country—whereas one would have become, for example, Muslim in North Africa—does not seem serious. It would be as frivolous, indeed, as being automatically Catholic, Orthodox, or Presbyterian because such is the family tradition. But to look among the religions for the one that seems most true amounts, basically, to curiosity. And what would be the result of this investigation, if one gave the pre-eminence to a given religion, for example to Christianity? What would be the nature of the faith one accorded it? The same as that which one accords, by joining it, to a political party? If one seeks a religion, one does not find God; one finds a religion. The motivation that launches the investigation determines its result. Beneath the apparent intellectual seriousness there lies a spiritual triviality.

And one may seek, finally, certainty and find oneself attracted by Christianity because of the all-encompassing explanatory power offered by the Bible or the Christian message. We all wish to discover the meaning of life, obscurely sensing that, despite so much randomness and misfortune, this meaning must exist and that its absence is scandalous, as if something had abusively deprived us of it. But certainty, once acquired, could be enough in itself, as a reward for the quest and an adequate response to the question. Perhaps one might wish, in the same spirit, to prove God's existence in order to clear away all doubt about it. However, if ever one happened upon a totally convincing proof—and Christians themselves have often endeavored to elaborate such proofs, as if the presentation of the gospel, of the good news, entailed them—one would find oneself in the presence, not of God, but of his logical counterfeit, of a simple product of language, of a thoroughly dazzling idea. The search for proofs, the very insistence that Christians furnish proofs in the name of human dignity, of intellectual honesty, amounts to placing oneself above God, by asking him to demonstrate that he exists. It is above all to be mistaken about the nature of God, who, being infinitely above us, reveals himself.

3.

At bottom, we do not know how to seek because of our nature and the fallen world that we inhabit. Yet it is precisely our estrangement from God, in a reality where he no longer speaks to us "in the cool of the day" (Genesis 3:8), that makes seeking necessary. And such is the compassion of God that even when going astray, even if we take one or the other of the mistaken ways of seeking that I have tried to identify, the quest may succeed, we may find ourselves face-to-face with the God who is "not willing that any should perish" (2 Peter 3:9), "who will have all men to be saved, and to come unto the knowledge of the truth" (1 Timothy 2:4). Still more astonishing texts, which direct our attention, not to ourselves and our problems, but to the nature of God. Even if our salvation is indifferent to us, it is important to God. Even if we do not know how to seek, God can teach us how.

Do we want to have faith? That is exactly what God wants.

But another barrier, properly demonic, looms between serious seeking and ourselves: the prestige of doubt. What could be more dangerous, we might think, than the conviction of possessing the truth, which provokes arrogance and intolerance and separates us from those who do not think as we do? Does it not easily slip, in religion, toward fundamentalism, fanaticism? What would become of open-mindedness and the availability of options if we were locked into a system of hard convictions? Do not soft convictions, resistance to indoctrination, better protect each one's liberty, the equality of all, and the fraternity of one with another? Is not doubt intellectually superior to certainty? Would it not be nobler, in short, to seek without finding?

Doubt is certainly wise and fertile in discovery in manifold circumstances. We know this; I acknowledged it in the chapter on faith. I add that in the presence of the revelation of God's truths, we find ourselves in the position of the great writer, as Keats describes him in a famous letter: by his "negative capability" he is "capable of being in uncertainties, mysteries, doubts, without any irritable reaching after fact and reason."[1] Confronted with Jesus's words at the Last Supper—"This is my body . . . this is my blood"—it is illusory to want to reason over the way the bread and the wine can be at the same time the body and the blood of Christ, to persist in trying to explain what is both clear and definitively mysterious. Concerning everything we read in the Bible, we may also doubt our interpretation in view of the gap between God's intelligence and ours, as well as the stupidity of sin that renders us incompetent to understand. However, it is not a matter of seeking convictions or assertions to brandish before others. One even discovers, in rereading the poem that is serving us here as guide, that the object of the search, curiously, is not elucidated. Jesus urges us to ask, to seek, and to knock at the door, but ask for what? Seek what? Knock where? It is as if he said: you do not know what to seek, open yourselves to what transcends you, let yourselves be guided, and you will learn little by little what is the goal of your search. The Gospel of Matthew follows these verses with a vigorous prose passage: "What man is there of you, whom if his son ask bread, will he give him a stone? Or if he ask a fish, will he give him a serpent? If ye then, being evil, know how to give good gifts unto your children, how

---

1 John Keats to Tom and George Keats, December 22, 1817, Poems by John Keats, accessed September 1, 2021, http://keats-poems.com/to-george-and-thomas-keats-hampstead-december-22-1817/.

much more shall your Father which is in heaven give good things to them that ask him!" (Matthew 7:9–11). Jesus indicates by familiar examples—bread, fish—that the search focuses on vital things; he reminds us, as in passing but in an abrupt and effective fashion, that we are "evil." In Luke's version, the passage ends thus: "How much more shall your heavenly Father give the Holy Spirit to them that ask him!" (Luke 11:11–13). The presence of the Holy Spirit (in place of "good gifts" in Matthew) is surprising, but it shows what, most essentially, we should ask of God: the Spirit, God himself, and how God will make the search possible by intervening in person to lead us on the right way.

4.

I am indeed eager to abandon all these subtly or grossly errant ways of seeking the correct way, to leave the human arguments doomed to vanity and focus on Jesus's words. What must one seek? Jesus. A person, and not an answer to philosophical questions. "Come unto me," he says, and not, "Concern yourself with religion, assure yourself first that God exists and then that he is the God of Christianity." In a sense, the invitation is too simple. It does not satisfy our desire for complexity, our need to be flattered by the intellectual effort demanded of us. Jesus humbles himself to the point of not speaking to us as a god, of telling us, "If any man thirst, let him come unto me"; "Come . . . I will give you rest." Confronted by this God who is too human for our pride, we are obliged to humble ourselves in our turn in order to grasp the nature of this totally simple search.

That Christianity is not a series of dogmas but a person is the ABC of Christian thought, but how difficult it is to concentrate on this fact and act accordingly! Everything changes, for the Christian as for the seeker, when one succeeds in so doing, but a seismic shift would be necessary for us all to do so together. And if the search is to succeed, it must be, for him who undertakes it, as I have said, of vital necessity. "Seek and ye shall find," if you desire it with all your being. "He that seeketh findeth," provided that finding becomes the goal of each day. If one can live without anguish while not searching, or at least without genuine disquiet, one will not find.

Unless, impatient in his love and escaping all our structures of thought, God manifests himself despite all that, despite ourselves.

And Jesus points out another dimension of the seriousness of the search. He invites us, with arms open on the cross, and he adds, aside from what he offers, what he asks. After the poem that I cited (Matthew 7:7–8), one comes upon this famous passage: "Enter ye in at the strait gate, . . . strait is the gate, and narrow is the way, which leadeth unto life, and few there be that find it" (Matthew 7:13–14). If Jesus does not speak these words immediately after the poem but on another occasion, Matthew, nevertheless, is guided to place them in such a way that we grasp the link between the two passages. In order to seek well, one must accept a certain constraint; for it to be opened, one must choose the narrow door. And then: "Seek and ye shall find [*eurèsete*] . . . few there be that find [*euriskontes*]"; by exhorting whomever to seek him, Jesus promises success to whoever accepts to do so, as he intends.

Similarly, after he cries, "Come unto me, all ye that are heavy laden, and I will give you rest" (Matthew 11:28), he immediately continues: "Take my yoke upon you, and learn of me; for I am meek and lowly in heart, and ye shall find rest unto your souls. For my yoke is easy, and my burden is light" (Matthew 11:29–30). He presents himself as a poor man, "meek and lowly in heart"— not as a master, even less as a god—while asking us to take on his yoke and, having found him, to follow him in obedience. Understood aright, one sees that he is proposing to lift a heavy burden (*pephor-tismenoi*, bowed under the burden) in exchange of a light (*phortion*)

burden. What precision in Jesus's words, in Matthew's writing!—
a precision that shapes their thought and causes us to ponder it.

And Jesus seems to go still further in his demands when he
substitutes, for the yoke and the burden, a cross: "And when he had
called the people unto him with his disciples also, he said unto them,
'Whosoever will come after me, let him deny himself, and take up
his cross, and follow me. For whosoever will save his life shall lose
it; but whosoever shall lose his life for my sake and the Gospel's,
the same shall save it'" (Mark 8:34–35). The cross one is to carry
recurs in all the Synoptic Gospels; the idea of losing one's life to
save it is also found in the Gospel of John (12:25). Jesus utters these
words on different occasions, and the Gospel writers repeat them with
emphasis, undoubtedly because they accompany, like their shadow,
the very generous and overwhelming invitations just to *ask, seek,
knock, come*. To take up one's cross, to lose one's life (an expression
whose depth I do not pretend to understand) is the ultimate proof
of the seriousness of our intention, a question for the seeker: does
he truly wish to find?

"He that hath ears to hear, let him hear!" is another expression
that also accompanies Jesus's apparently easily grasped calls, and it
is spread broadly in the Gospels. It generally closes allegorical para-
bles and figurative teachings whose meanings have to be discovered,
but it seems also reasonable to relate it to these calls. Just what does
one hear in reading, "Seek and ye shall find"; "Come unto me"? Is one
able to receive these words such as Jesus intends them? Above all,
do we have the proper ears to grasp their true meaning and what is
at stake for us in them? If Jesus draws our attention to his person,
the fabulous end of our desire, these other more troubling words
oblige the would-be seeker to reflect on his own condition, on what,
in himself, may prevent him from hearing. They make him examine
himself, his insufficiency, his lack, his exclusion from the good, the
true, and the beautiful.

For Jesus—who appears everywhere as the one who gives, opens, comforts—does not begin his teaching this way. What are his very first words in the Gospel of Mark? "The time is fulfilled, and the kingdom of God is at hand: repent ye, and believe the Gospel" (Mark 1:15). The same first words in the Gospel of Matthew (after those he says to John the Baptist at his baptism, then to the devil at his temptation in the wilderness): "Jesus began to preach, and to say, 'Repent: for the kingdom of heaven is at hand'" (Matthew 4:17). From the beginning, it is about repentance, and even before Jesus's preaching: according to Mark, John the Baptist had already proclaimed "the baptism of repentance for the remission of sins" (Mark 1:4); for Matthew, the same words of the Baptist, "Repent ye: for the kingdom of heaven is at hand" (Matthew 3:2), had announced those of Jesus. When Jesus sends the twelve disciples on a mission to proclaim, they too, that "the kingdom of heaven is at hand" (Matthew 10:7), "they went out," says Mark, "and preached that men should repent" (Mark 6:12). The necessity of repentance continues to be emphasized in the Gospels, and the first Christian sermon after Jesus's messages, that of Peter addressing the "men of Israel" on the day of Pentecost (Acts 2:22), ends—when his listeners, "pricked in their hearts" (Acts 2:37), ask him what they must do—in these words: "Repent, and be baptized every one of you in the name of Jesus Christ for the remission of sins" (Acts 2:38).

The call to repentance is initially addressed to the Jews, in a direct line from the Old Testament prophets' exhortations. It then extends to all. Jesus shows his disciples, after the resurrection, that according to the Scriptures, the Christ would rise from the dead "and that repentance and remission of sins should be preached in his name among all nations" (Luke 24:47). Paul ends his speech before the Areopagus of Athens by declaring that God "now commandeth all men everywhere to repent" (Acts 17:30).

The message of the meek and mild Jesus can prove to be hard. To seek, to come to Jesus implies repenting of what we are and desiring to change.

That is the meaning of the verb *metanoeô*: to repent, to change one's mind and sentiments in view of another way of behaving, to accomplish a radical transformation. "Seek and ye shall find" means "seek to know the Other and agree to become another person yourself." To pass from openness and vulnerability in the invitation to *seek* to the strict and troublesome command to *repent* can certainly distress us, but here is what Paul says to each of his readers in Rome: "The goodness of God leadeth thee to repentance" (Romans 2:4). It is God who leads us to repent by making us the object of his goodness. Once again, God precedes us, the initiative comes from him, a divine act of which we are unaware draws us. God wants us more than we want him.

Repentance is mysterious. It participates in that immense process of change that animates history between the fall and the end of time; change in the individual, who receives a "heart of flesh" in place of a "stony heart" (Ezekiel 11:19); change in the Christian at the moment of his entrance into the Kingdom of God, in "a moment, in the twinkling of an eye" (1 Corinthians 15:52); change of the entire universe into "new heavens and a new earth" (2 Peter 3:13, etc.); change from the crucifixion to the resurrection, from death to life, from sadness to joy. Once again, the search is serious, the demands sobering, if one desires to change and, as soon as one realizes who one is and what one does, to be pardoned.

The moment that someone opens the door and the seeker passes over the threshold to find he knows not what is outside of time, or rather, an instant in time finds itself penetrated, permeated, fulfilled, by the intervention of eternity. Later, he will understand that God had been at work for a long time, as Pascal writes in an unforgettable paradox that he puts in the mouth of God addressing the new convert: "You would not be seeking me if you had not found me" (*Pensées*, "The Mystery of Jesus").

Creatures of God, we continue to live thanks to him, as the entire universe is maintained by his creative power continually renewed. Paul puts this memorably in his speech before the Athenian Areopagus: God is not far from each of us, for in him "we live and move and have our being" (Acts 17:28). One might prefer a translation even closer to the concise power of the Greek: *en autô gar zômen kai kinoumetha kai esmen*, "for in him we live and move and are." It is in God that we *are*, always-already, whether we know it or not, whether this pleases us or not.

The formula translates or captures a living, dynamic ontology. What precedes it plunges us into a very palpably lived experience. God created men, says Paul, to live on the face of the earth, "that they should seek the Lord, if haply they might feel after him, and find him" (Acts 17:27). The search for God is feeling one's way; according to the Greek word that Paul chooses—*psèlaphaô*, a verb—one even gropes blindly, like a blind man in the dark. (It is what the Cyclops in Homer's *Odyssey* does after losing his eye.) To seek God is to feel about oneself in the dark ("with one's hand," according to the Port-Royal translation), the whole person being engaged in an action that is far from being intellectual only.

In using the same words as Jesus—seek, find—Paul speaks in realistic fashion of our confusion, our dissatisfaction, our intuition of *something else*, putting himself at the level of our poverty. We need not aspire to the absolute, to the sacred, nor choose a religion, nor torture our brains weighing the numerous "proofs" of God's existence. In our weakness, we simply have to feel our way forward, like the blind people we are.

5.

And how to seek? By reading the Bible. This seems obvious: if one is seeking God, what could be more normal than to listen to his word? If one desires faith, is it not fitting to examine the book that presents it and offers it? Yet Christians do not always think spontaneously of giving this advice, having other things in mind: "dialogue," the apologetic tradition, and so forth. It is the same deviation, the same refusal of the essential as when one substitutes, for believers, religious duties for the knowledge of God. Since one must seek, not the truth of Christianity, but Christ himself, the privileged intermediaries are first of all the Scriptures, the word of God that reveals the Word of God, and then Christians who read them and can make them understood.

Our Western culture's influence over us and our embarrassment at the idea of entering into contact with a supernatural person are frightening.

It is dangerous to read the Bible. The Spirit who speaks in it transcends us absolutely, and how can one know what he is going to require? However, if one is sincere, one listens to it and understands it. As it already understands us. And Pascal, who—captive to seventeenth-century rationalism and despite his so very important conviction of the role of the heart in the knowledge of the real and singularly of God—spoke of the "proofs of Jesus Christ" and wanted to show that the Christian religion is "venerable" and deserving of respect. I rejoice that he wrote the following in his Memorial, when he found himself at the heart and at the summit of his faith in "fire" and "tears of joy":

Forgetfulness of the world and of everything, except God.
He is only found by the ways taught in the Gospel.

This is exactly what Jesus says. At the end of the parable of the rich man and the poor man who die and find themselves, the former in Hades and the latter in "Abraham's bosom," the rich man asks Abraham to send the poor man to his five brothers to spare them the torments he is suffering by urging them to repent. Abraham replies, "If they hear not Moses and the prophets, neither will they be persuaded, though one rose from the dead" (Luke 16:31). Even the testimony to the afterlife of someone risen from the dead—a testimony a thousand times more striking than any "proof"—could not persuade those who do not listen to the Scriptures; the only way for the brothers to be saved would be to read them and follow their injunctions. The parable (which in the first place concerns charity) is addressed first to the Jews, to those who are not willing to hear what is for us the Old Testament. But it also applies to unbelievers now and to seekers, for whom the royal way to God, to Jesus, passes through the Old Testament and the New.

Finally, to know that faith is a gift of God, who gives it or not, does not mean that we can only wait in trembling but that we do not seek alone and in a sort of void. God also is at work. It is he who takes the initiative; it is he who seeks us, even before we think of seeking. He asks, in the Old Testament, "Have I any pleasure at all that the wicked should die? . . . and not that he should return from his ways, and live?" (Ezekiel 18:23). Jesus affirms, in the New, concerning the lost sheep, "Even so it is not the will of your Father which is in heaven, that one of these little ones should perish" (Matthew 18:14). Not one.

And God, in the person of Jesus, knows weakness; the All-Powerful experiences powerlessness. In a passage that recurs in each of the Synoptic Gospels, the high priests, the scribes, the elders, seeing Jesus nailed on the cross, mock him, saying, "He saved others; himself he cannot save!" (Matthew 27:42; Mark 15:31) or "Let him save himself!" (Luke 23:35). If one must not forget that Jesus sacrifices himself of his own free will—"I lay down my life. / . . . No man taketh it from me, / but I lay it down of myself" (John 10:17–18)— for love of his Father and for love of us, then he could not come down from the cross. And, once "forsaken" by God (Matthew 27:46; Mark 15:34) and separated from him, apparently, by the weight of all the sins of the world that he had to bear in our place, he trusted in his Father to raise him. The powerlessness to which Jesus consented, with the resurrection that followed, is the most inspiring and reassuring reason not to despair because of our inability to believe, to reach God, to serve him.

After the thousands of words of this chapter that are almost all mine, after these reasonings of a European intellectual, I prefer to close in quoting anew Jesus's poem with which I began, sublime and yet so close to us:

Ask, and it shall be given you;
Seek, and ye shall find;
Knock, and it shall be opened unto you:
For every one that asketh receiveth;
And he that seeketh findeth;
And to him that knocketh it shall be opened.

10

I Am the Truth

Writing on the Bible always poses a certain danger for oneself and for the reader. It is easy to deform revelation, through blindness, through conformism to one or another tradition, or through the impulses of our fallen nature. Revelation comes from a God who transcends us infinitely, and certain passages of the Bible are particularly mysterious. Nevertheless, they prompt us to explore them in order to go beyond ourselves. So in this final chapter, I propose to examine a statement in the gospel that is as difficult to gaze at as the sun and even further beyond our reach, for I consider it essential if we wish to come back to the truth of Christianity. It once again concerns Jesus.

And after all, the Bible encourages us everywhere to accomplish precisely what we are incapable of: to believe in God, to love God, to love our neighbor, "to will and to do" what God wills (Philippians 2:13). To act as one cannot, to be what one cannot: this is the requirement and the strange promise of Christianity.

1.

Jesus announces to the disciples that he is going to leave and that "whither I go ye know, and the way ye know." Thomas having maintained that they know neither where he is going nor the way he is taking, Jesus answers him, "I am the way, the truth, and the life" (John 14:4–6). A famous sentence, clear and abstruse at the same time and, above all, revolutionary. We would have understood if Jesus had declared, "I show the way, I say the truth, I give the life." With the sentence as it is, we are entirely disoriented by such simple words: "I am the truth." The truth, which raises us toward the universal, toward the abstract, which convinces us, after vigorous research, of the nature of the, shall we say, material world, which inspires us as an idea, as an ideal, in so many domains of thought and creativity, how can it be constituted by a person? Is not the expression "I am the truth" an abuse of language, the production of a signified as unreal as a triangular thought? And if we believe it, what fundamental disruption of our ways of thinking must we expect?

It is the "I" that disconcerts us. It is even underlined in John's Greek: "Egô eimi hè hodos kai hè alètheia kai hè zôè," where the presence of the word *egô*, which the Greek could dispense with in saying "I am," calls in English for "*I* am the way." We seek the way, we want the truth, and we aspire to life, and Jesus affirms that he himself is all of that, that he does not just hold the key. Viewed from here, it is unreasonable, impossible. Either he is the Son of God, with a revelation that no one could have foreseen, or he is deranged.

If we take his laconic and dense words seriously, they guide us to this fact of capital importance: Christianity is not a religion, but a person. We know this, as we know, if we believe John's Gospel, that Jesus is the truth. But we forget this when we think of the

Christian life or of evangelism. For whoever is outside Christianity, such ideas appear absurd, not at all in keeping with what one may expect from a religion, and totally foreign to the normal way of seeing things.

Indeed, Jesus's little sentence sweeps away all our representations of truth. We in the West have developed a set of admirable rules for determining *what is*, as opposed to *what is not*, particularly logical reasoning and the verification of hypotheses. They are only relatively trustworthy, since they may lead us into error. The ontological arguments for the existence of God "prove," according to an internal articulation without any hold on the real, the existence of a Being of reason bearing no relation to the true God. (They distance us, above all, from *knowing* God in Jesus.) The most exacting scientists know that their results are always susceptible to being modified by other data or by a new theory. "I am the truth"—words come from beyond, oblige us to conceive truth in another way, by indicating the gap between our perspective and that of God and by presenting Jesus, in his person, as the intermediary, both fearful to us and near. It is impertinent, in both the modern and earlier senses of the word, and frankly ridiculous, to wish to reason about the existence of God or to verify the elements of a revelation, and the only way to assure oneself that Jesus is the truth is to know him.

In transcending our conceptions of truth, Jesus does not call them into question; he distances them, he leaves them in their place. And he does not destroy the notion of an objective truth; on the contrary, he reinforces it. In an era when, to the minds of many, nothing *is*—everything is modifiable, everything is an appearance created by a point of view, from the "real" (which is not real) to history, morality, or the individual—he constitutes in himself objective truth, an incommensurable Real that resists us by its strong presence.

Jesus's forever astonishing words should persuade us once and for all that Christianity does not present itself as a combination of doctrines, a system of thought. Christians constantly forget this. Since theology has become in spite of all a summa of propositions, an incessant word between the Bible and us, they feel the need to defend theological discourse according to criteria proposed by various purely human theories of truth. Beginning with the obligation placed on us by the Bible to be always ready to give an answer for the hope within us (1 Peter 3:15), even Pierre Manent assumes (in a collective work titled *Qu'est-ce que la vérité?*) that the believer must present "his reasons for believing, first in *a* God, then in *this* God." What would Saint Peter say of a Christian who found it important, before speaking of the saving God he has encountered, to elaborate an argument in favor of the existence of this abstraction, unknown to the Bible but quite European: "a God"? Even Urs von Balthasar sought to "make the Christian message credible and acceptable to the world." What would Saint Paul say of this appeal to the wisdom of men that is nothing, in God's sight, but a "folly" (1 Corinthians 1:20)? And why does one not ask oneself this kind of question continually?

Could it be because we do not read the Bible enough and we do not have the habit of checking our assertions, when we reflect on a given Christian subject, by referring to biblical truth?

The first and ultimate truth is Jesus, and if our mind admits its impotence before the strange immensity of such a mystery, we may at least appreciate the emotion of the apostle John, in wonderment at having *encountered the truth*. He who alone reports this affirmation by Jesus (as he reports a whole series of other affirmations beginning with the words "I am") says also on the subject of the Word, "We beheld his glory, the glory as of the only begotten of the Father, full of grace and truth" (John 1:14) and declares that, if the Law was given through Moses, "Grace and truth came by Jesus Christ" (John 1:17). It is also John who describes the scene where Pilate asks Jesus, standing before him, "What is truth?" (John 18:38), a striking moment to which I will return, and who affirms concerning the Spirit, in a grammatical construction as absolute as that of Jesus, that he "is truth" (*to pneuma estin hè alètheia*; 1 John 5:6). John had seen the truth appear in the world in the traits of a man; he had contemplated it and, to quote the terms he uses in referring to Jesus, "the Word of life," he had heard and touched it with his hands (1 John 1:1). He was constantly astonished by this truth that was walking around Palestine. The words translated by *truth* and by *true* recur much more often in his Gospel than the others, as if the vision of the truth incarnate never left him.

2.

Jesus is the foreign truth—foreign to a race adulterated by sin—which came into the world, unveiled itself in Palestine, and is still unveiling itself. This truth is other; it is beyond logic, beyond proof, beyond verification unless by means of knowing, of a reciprocal experience. Michel Henry understood this clearly in an impressive book, *I Am the Truth*, published in 1996.[1] There he postulates that a "radical difference" separates "the Truth of Christianity from that of the world" (35), and he presents "the Christian concept of truth" as "irreducible to the concept of truth that dominates the history of Western thought, from Greece to contemporary phenomenology," this traditional concept determining even "the idea one has today of truth in the domain of scientific knowledge as in that of common sense" (36). This is forcefully said; one could simply question the term "Christian *concept* of truth," a nonbiblical notion borrowed precisely from the philosophy that is here rejected. He also sees "the massive misinterpretation that reduces

---

1 Michel Henry, *C'est moi la vérité: Pour une philosophie du christianisme* (Paris: Éditions du Seuil, 1996).

the essence of the Christian God to Being and thus to a concept of Greek thought" and the blight of the "great Western theologies" that, starting from this concept, "reduce the God of Abraham to that of the philosophers and scholars" (41).

Yet while conscious of the gap between the truth of Jesus and our ways of elaborating theologies and philosophies, Henry is such a captive of his university discipline that he succeeds despite everything in integrating this truth into a very Western way of thinking. Working on a new version of phenomenology ("substituting one phenomenology for another"; 109), he maintains that the entire philosophical system is inoperable before the alterity of a revealed truth—except one of its contemporary forms. He writes, for example, concerning Christ as intermediary between God and men, "What this role of 'intermediary' consists of: this is what a phenomenology of life allows us to grasp in a radicality to which no other form of thought, for lack of appropriate means, was able to rise" (138). One must believe that not only the successive theologians but the authors also of the New Testament made commendable efforts to understand, but for lack of means . . . He even seems to deem that the Bible foresees, and uses, phenomenological thought—related to the Truth: "The Way expresses then a general thesis of phenomenology, namely that the way of access to a given thing consists in the manifestation of that thing" (159). The word of Jesus—"I am the way, the truth, and the life"—reveals the salutary gulf between all our intellectual habits and a reality that transcends us; Henry, having shown this with brio, erases that gulf by ceaselessly deploying the theses and terminology of his own philosophy. Finally, according to him, Western thought is not altogether without resources, for there exists a renovated phenomenology.

Here is the problem; the clearest vision of the dissimilarity of the biblical word does not prevent us from hanging on to our own ways of reasoning, as if we really did not want to submit our intelligence to what is beyond us. Whence the danger of letting ourselves be led into error, of developing arguments from paradigms of our system of thought that contradict, *without our realizing it*, the declarations of the Bible. The Bible itself is depreciated, for example, if we think ourselves capable of judging it according to our theory of language. The words of Christ, according to Henry, "are only, in the text of the Gospels, . . . moments and parts of a language, of a word, only ever being able to add a meaning to a meaning, without ever spanning the abyss that separates all signifying truth from the reality signified by it" (14). Those texts, whatever might be "the respect with which they are surrounded . . . are only, in spite of all, texts" (13). "A milieu of pure unreality," the language is "foreign to life" (211). My experience as a poet leads me to reject this Saussurean notion of language in general; reading Paul's second letter to Timothy could convince us in particular of the totally different status of the biblical texts: "All scripture is given by inspiration of God" (2 Timothy 3:16). It is true that the words of the Bible are not precisely what persuades us of the truth of God but rather the Holy Spirit who speaks to us in those words; if God does not reveal himself, the text of the Bible remains, for us, a dead letter. However, if we *hear* what the Bible says, we feel at our level the divine power in it, we grasp its difference compared to all other writing, without exception. It is not just a matter of reading texts, but of hearing a word, spoken by someone in the present moment of listening. The Bible addresses the ear of the heart in order for us to hear above all the words of Jesus. Otherwise, the exhortation he repeats with fervor—"Who hath ears to hear let him hear!"—would only have had any meaning during his years of preaching and for a few of his contemporaries. That the Bible is revelation is not demonstrable but audible.

3.

And the truth is not alone. It participates in a triple reality by offering itself at the same time as the way and the life. Here is the other surprise in Jesus's declaration: the question Thomas asks him concerns only the way; his answer adds the truth and the life in a series of words that rhetoric would call a gradation. The *way* deepens (if I am not mistaken) into *truth* and the truth into *life*. Jesus often answers like this, going beyond what one expects, speaking to the side or introducing, as with Nicodemus, an unforeseeable and fathomless idea: "Verily . . . except a man be born again, he cannot see the kingdom of God" (John 3:3). (In only a score of verses, the encounter with Nicodemus constitutes one of the most singular and most touching conversations ever to have taken place.) Here, having unveiled an unsuspected world by affirming, "I am the way," he unveils others, those of the truth and of the life, which are still more vast. Reading the Bible, a humanly divine word, always produces a comparable effect: everything is enlarged around us, the finite world opens onto the infinite.

It is possible that John captures in his writing this alterity of the word of the Word, the disciples speaking in prose and Jesus, if not in verse, in a sovereignly rhythmical prose.

As the words "I am the truth" sweep away our habitual conceptions of the nature of truth, of the search for it, and of the ways of demonstrating it, so "I am the way" rules out all the known ways of following a path. Properly understood, Jesus asks more of us than to imitate him. If one must assuredly seek to act, to think, to be like him ("Let this mind be in you, which was also in Christ Jesus," Philippians 2:5), we are urged especially to walk *in* him, to live his life in us. Whence the mysterious affirmation in a passage of Paul's letter to the Galatians, which I have often commented on without succeeding in perfectly understanding it: "I live; yet not I, but Christ liveth in me" (Galatians 2:20). Another text, more or less well known, but which too often disappears when we think of the priorities of religious life. Probably because we are disconcerted to realize the distance that separates the experience of Paul, who has no hesitation to speak this way, from ours.

The way that leads to Christ is Christ. He is also the way that leads to the Father. Jesus has just announced to the disciples that he is going away to prepare a place in his Father's house for them; immediately after the sentence that concerns us, he adds, "No man cometh unto the Father, but by me" (John 14:6). In this quite simple perspective, it is not essentially a matter of believing in Christianity, of belonging to a given church, of performing religious duties, but of going toward the Father by the only possible way. It is remarkable also that, at the very moment when Jesus says "I," with emphasis on the word, he is in reality effacing himself in favor of the Father. As Paul effaced himself in favor of the Christ living within him, having "this mind . . . which was also in Christ Jesus" (Philippians 2:5).

This announcement of the true way, and that of the true truth, arrives from somewhere outside the world that our intelligences could not have reached. The announcement of the true life as well. All our ideas of what life is pale before a Life that is presented as a Person; writing about this encroaches upon holy ground, for we are dealing with the life of God. It is unimaginable; it is offered to us. Hence the apparently insane words that serve to put us in touch with it. Certain passages in Paul's letters, though familiar, astonish us indeed, once we grasp how radically they change our vision of things—once, by listening attentively, we *hear* them. What is the condition of humans on earth? "If one died for all, then were all dead" (2 Corinthians 5:14). All humanity, quite alive in flesh and bone, in intelligence and sensibility, is in fact, in the perspective of the true life, dead. The remedy is just as unexpected and foreign to the distinctions that our method of thinking establishes. In order to escape death, one must "be born again" (John 3:3), be "born of the Spirit" (John 3:6), find oneself among those who are "born . . . of God" (John 1:13). And if, following this spiritual and super-human birth, we live a life that is also other, "as those that are alive from the dead" (Romans 6:13), that is when the frightening opposite of life comes back: "Ye are dead," writes Paul to the Colossians, "and your life is hid with Christ in God" (Colossians 3:3). Christians, too, the only ones alive, are dead, and the unthinkable paradox leads to that inexhaustible passage already quoted: "I live; yet not I, but Christ liveth in me" (Galatians 2:20). In order to live this life, divine in origin, that is given to us, we are obliged to efface ourselves completely and recognize that insofar as life is indeed in us, it is that of Another. In the same way that we need a new birth, we need a new death.

Reading these passages one after the other makes one dizzy and clearly demonstrates the divine foreignness of what is proposed.

4.

The new truth that Jesus is thus extends to the way and above all the life. Its nature can be a little better understood when Jesus refers, speaking with Nicodemus, to the one "that doeth the truth" (John 3:21). Placing the truth in the domain of action, he steers us away from the truth as a preoccupation of the intellect and as a concept. He returns to the point of view of the Old Testament, in which "to walk" in the truth of God defines, repeatedly, the way of life that is demanded of the faithful. His formula is also found in the first epistle of John, which holds that "if we . . . walk in darkness, we lie, and do not the truth" (1 John 1:6). To do the truth rather than to think it recovers the Hebrew perspective on the true and immerses us in a world where the Greek idea appears inadequate, despite the fact that it is the word *alètheia* that is repeated each time.

It is often maintained that the Greek term spreads throughout the New Testament its presuppositions, as one of the signs of a reconciliation between Hebrew and Hellenistic thought, a reconciliation so greatly desired by certain of the first Christian commentators, who were not very disposed to venture beyond the culture in which they had been brought up. Would it not be more in accord with the Scriptures to recognize that the Hebrew context, and above all Jesus's declaration affirming that he is himself the truth, give the word *alètheia* a new meaning—evangelizes it, as it were? This is clearly seen by rereading what Jesus says to Nicodemus: "Everyone that doeth evil hateth the light . . . but he that doeth truth cometh to the light" (John 3:20–21). If the distinction between truth and untruth certainly figures in the Bible, Jesus here opposes the truth to evil, thus assimilating the truth to the good—not to the idea of the good but to the good that is done.

Nicodemus must remain once again perplexed, if he expects, like the reader of John, the expression "that doeth evil" to be contrasted with "that doeth good." The same redefinition of *truth* applies when Jesus says to certain Jews who have believed him that by abiding in his word, they will be his disciples and, he continues, "Ye shall know the truth, and the truth shall make you free" (John 8:32). We have taken up these words to give them a meaning that is convenient for us and corresponds to our idea of progress: the development of knowledge will free us from our religious and political prejudices and allow us the better to live together. Jesus speaks differently. His interlocutors needed to be freed from the "sin" of which they were "the servant[s]" (John 8:34), and the knowledge that they are offered is existential. They will not know propositional truths (or not primarily those); they will know Jesus, and becoming "truly" his disciples, they will live the truth in their relationship with God and others. They will *know* the truth as one *knows* a woman. John emphasizes the reality of this knowledge, which one attains only by living in a certain manner, making the knowledge of the truth (*alètheia*) depend on being truly (*alèthôs*) a disciple of Jesus. A sublime tautology: in behaving according to the truth, one experiences the truth. I even sense that John is happy, translating the words of Jesus into Greek, to be able to write, for "the truth shall make you free"—*hè alètheia eleutherôsei humas*, the play of sonorities between *alètheia* and *eleutherôsei* suggesting that truth and freedom go hand in hand.

It is a question, before being able to act in conformity with the truth, of *being* according to the truth. Already in the Old Testament, in the course of the model of confession that Psalm 51 comprises, David addresses God in this way: "Thou desirest truth in the inward parts" (Psalm 51:6). In the new perspective offered by Jesus, we may understand: you love Jesus in the depths of our being. (It is often possible to substitute *Jesus* for *truth*. For example, "If ye . . . then are truly my disciples . . . ye shall know *me*.") It is again John, and he alone, who on this subject uses a particularly important expression. "Let us not love," he writes in his first epistle, "in word, neither in tongue; but in deed and in truth. And hereby we know that we are of the truth" (1 John 3:18–19). In his Gospel, Jesus uses the same expression: "Every one that is of the truth heareth my voice" (John 18:37). Here he is speaking to Pilate, who cannot hear him, not so much because Jesus's words are beyond him, but because he is not "of the truth." Jesus has already spoken in these terms to hostile listeners: "Ye believe not, because ye are not of my sheep, as I said unto you. My sheep hear my voice" (John 10:26–27). To be "of the truth" is to have been made capable, by a power outside our power, of hearing the divine word, the voice of Jesus. Whence the drama of evangelism: listeners hear if they are of the truth, if they are "sheep" even unknowingly, or they do not hear. And it is not arguments, proofs that make the difference. The truth is always revealed, God convinces us of his presence—and not the logic of his existence—and the proof lies in what we experience. However, it is not a matter of a purely subjective conviction; to the contrary, what could be more objective than this encounter with the alterity of the biblical word and with Another?

5.

"What is truth?" asks Pilate, without understanding that it is before his very eyes. Jesus gives him the response, "*I* am the truth," by his simple presence. Pilate, of course, does not hear him, for Jesus has already told him, implicitly, that he is not capable of hearing him, not being "of the truth." If he seeks it without seeing it in front of him, it is because he is excluded from it.

Pilate's question is ours, from generation to generation. He seems to have posed it with a certain degree of fear, for when the Jews indicate that Jesus proclaims himself the Son of God, he is "the more afraid" (John 19:8). We too should ask the question of truth with fear and trembling. The truth does not belong to us, and the most radical questions, on the ultimate significance of human life and of the universe, call for answers that are situated above our means. The sum of our truths does not give us access to the supreme truth; the sciences, which admirably demonstrate the *what* and the *how*, are powerless before the *why* and become absurd if they claim to have proven that the *why* does not exist. Truth is strange.

If we ask fundamental questions about our condition, about the essential truth, it is because we find ourselves in a fallen world, separated through our own fault from a God who loves us. We do not know the answers to our questions because we have willed to know evil. Our seeking can end only in Jesus, who is Truth itself and who, far from being a simple answer—how could God, who preexists everything, follow our questions?—immeasurably enlarges the nature of the truth, the individual, and the reality in which the latter awakens. Our lot is to desire and seek the truth and to recognize, when the truth finds us, that it shows itself to be abnormal, inexhaustible, literally infinite, and to our great happiness, impossible to envelop in our thought and our language. It is to be feared that our modernity is greatly distanced from it, and one of Isaiah's observations clarifies our misfortune: "Truth is fallen in the street. . . . Yea, truth faileth" (Isaiah 59:14–15). But it is not too late; the promise is there. The truth is not primarily that God exists, that he created the universe, that he sent his Son to help us, that Jesus died for our sins and rose for our salvation—even though all that is certainly the case and perfectly true. The truth is Jesus as the Son of God. One finds the truth little by little by walking with Jesus and in him, as one finds it in letting the life of Jesus be in us. The words "I am the truth" are not only an assertion; they arrive as an invitation. If Jesus is the Truth indeed, he is also the truth for us.